BEYOND LONELINESS

Books by Elizabeth Skoglund

Beyond Loneliness

Elizabeth Skoglund

A *Doubleday-Galilee Original*

DOUBLEDAY & COMPANY, INC., GARDEN CITY, NEW YORK, 1980

6771

ISBN: 0-385-13192-5
Library of Congress Catalog Card Number 78-73194
Copyright © 1980 by Elizabeth Skoglund

The patients mentioned in this book are real, and their stories are true. However, to protect their privacy, names and other identifying details have been changed.

All Biblical quotations, unless otherwise noted, are from *The Living Bible*. Copyright © 1971 by Tyndale House Publishers, Wheaton, Illinois 60187. Used by permission.

Permission to quote from the following sources is gratefully acknowledged: GOLD BY MOONLIGHT, by Amy Carmichael, Fort Washington, Pa., Christian Literature Crusade, 1970, used by permission of Christian Literature Crusade; KOHILA, by Amy Carmichael, Fort Washington, Pa., Christian Literature Crusade, used by permission of Christian Literature Crusade; *The Cocktail Party*, by T. S. Eliot, New York, Harcourt Brace, copyright © 1950 by T. S. Eliot; THE PURSUIT OF MEANING: LOCAL THERAPY, VIKTOR FRANKL AND YOU, Harper & Row, copyright © 1980 by Joseph B. Fabry; THE WILL TO MEANING, by Viktor E. Frankl © 1969 by Viktor E. Frankl, reprinted by arrangement with The New American Library, Inc., New York, N.Y.; MRS. HOWARD TAYLOR, HER WEB OF TIME, by Joy Guinness, London, Lutterworth Press, Ltd., 1952, copyright © 1952 by China Inland Mission (now known as the Overseas Missionary Fellowship); LETTERS TO AN AMERICAN LADY, by C. S. Lewis, Grand Rapids, Mich., Wm. B. Eerdmans Publishing Company, 1967, used by permission; MERE CHRISTIANITY, by C. S. Lewis, Geoffrey Bles, Ltd., London and New York, reprinted with permission of Macmillan Publishing Company, Inc., copyright © 1943, 1945, 1952, by Macmillan Publishing Company, Inc.; "Friendship," from THE FOUR LOVES, by C. S. Lewis, reprinted with permission of Harcourt Brace; GIFT FROM THE SEA, by Anne Morrow Lindbergh, © 1965 by Anne Morrow Lindbergh, reprinted by permission, Bantam Books, a Division of Random House, Inc.; A MAN CALLED PETER, by Catherine Marshall, copyright 1951 by Catherine Marshall, published by Chosen Books, Lincoln,

To G. L. Harrington, M.D.

Contents

Foreword

In seventeenth-century England, before the harshness of the Industrial Revolution had begun, John Donne wrote his famous words:

No man is an island entire of itself; every man is a piece of the continent, a part of the main. . . . Any man's death diminishes me, because I am involved in mankind, and therefore never send to know for whom the bell tolls; it tolls for thee.[1]

Positive, but not entirely realistic; for as the bleakness of the Industrial Revolution set in with all its philosophical disillusionment and economic deprivation, men did indeed feel like islands, isolated and lonely.

In the words of Matthew Arnold, a poet of that era:

> . . . in the sea of life enisled,
> With echoing straits between us thrown,
> Dotting the shoreless watery wild,
> We mortal millions live *alone*.[2]

A contemporary statement of the same idea can be found in T. S. Eliot's *The Cocktail Party:*

> . . . Hell is oneself,
> Hell is alone, the other figures in it

Merely projections. There is nothing to escape from
And nothing to escape to. One is always alone.[3]

In truth we are all alone in this world. Ultimately no one
can get inside of our skin and be us—or live for us, or suffer
for us. But perhaps neither John Donne nor T. S. Eliot was
correct; for while we *are* in a sense islands, alone, to be alone
is *not* Hell. To be alone does not even mean one has to be
lonely.

For in our attempts to alleviate loneliness we have tried to
deny it, spiritualize it, embrace it, and finally we have given
up altogether with a sense of confusion and defeat.

Defeat is not, however, the ultimate end of our endeavors.
For, while loneliness cannot be eradicated, it can be understood in a way that enables a person to live beyond a constant, nagging sense of loneliness.

To be lonely is not to be emotionally ill. It does not indicate
pathology with deep-seated causes. It indicates humanness,
not sinfulness. It is human to be lonely, but it is not necessary
to succumb to the feelings.

It is therefore from the viewpoint of the normal that this
book has been written. For in the view of the author, loneliness is less the disease of this century than it is a general but
surmountable condition of mankind.

Elizabeth Skoglund
1979

NOTES

1. John Donne, "Meditation 17," from *Devotions upon Emergent
   Occasions,* in Robert P. Tristram Coffin and Alexander M. With-

erspoon, eds., *Seventeenth Century Prose* (New York: Harcourt
Brace Jovanovich, 1929, 1946), p. 68.

2. Matthew Arnold, *Dover Beach,* in George Benjamin Woods
and Jerome Hamilton Buckley, *Poetry of the Victorian Period*
(Chicago: Scott, Foresman & Company, 1955), p. 483.

3. T. S. Eliot, *The Cocktail Party* (New York: Harcourt Brace
Jovanovich, 1950).

BEYOND LONELINESS

1

A Bridge over Troubled Waters

NOT LONG AGO, I sat in a restaurant above one of the most beautiful bays in the world, Zihuatanejo Bay, in Mexico. My companion and I were outside, and the tropical heat of the day had become modified to a gentle warmth. As darkness spread over the bay, a newspaperman from the States, whom I had just met, excused himself to put one of his tapes on the stereo that the restaurant's owner played from time to time. "Bridge Over Troubled Water" blared out. Bill looked at me quietly and said, "Isn't that why we're all here?"

At our table was a travel-jaded woman who spends about ten months out of twelve in Mexico and South America. A newlywed couple were spending a month in this charming little town after saving their money for two years. A secretary from the States, an American student, and a Mexican student from Mexico City completed our number. We were different from each other. At home we might never even have wanted to spend an evening together. But Bill was right. In one way or another we had each gone to this small, primitive but peaceful little town to find our bridge.

For most of us, the bridge was from the rat race and depersonalization of American society. We talked late into the
night. We exposed our inner thoughts. We trusted and took
time to understand each other. We were in a remote spot of
the world, but we were not lonely. We had all come from a
life where loneliness is epitomized by a fear of not being understood. Here it was different. We had time, and, even more,
we were safe, as a group of travelers who would probably
never meet again, to face all that had been said. In the words
of the English poet Matthew Arnold:

> I knew the mass of men concealed
> Their thoughts, for fear that if revealed
> They would by other men be met
> With blank indifference, or with blame reproved. . . .[1]

Yet, admits Arnold,

> The same heart beats in every breast![2]

Arnold goes on in the same poem to fantasize the enormous
relief if even for a moment we can be free, honest, and understood by another human being. Then he says:

> . . . an unwonted calm pervades his breast.
> And then he thinks he knows
> The hills where his life rose,
> And the sea where it goes.[3]

Loneliness has been a timeless problem, affected by the current history of any society and yet present in life at all times
of recorded history. After all of his family have been destroyed and all of his friends have misunderstood his pain,
Job, in the Old Testament, cries out, "Though He slay me, yet
will I trust Him," in reference to Jehovah (Job 13:15, King

James Version). His loneliness lay in the desolation of a righteous man suffering because he *was* righteous and being told by his "friends" to confess his sins so that prosperity and companionship could once again be his.

Job lived thousands of years ago in a country remote from ours. But in my office in the United States today, I still hear the same cause and feeling of loneliness from people who hurt and then are made to feel guilty for that hurt. "Confess your depression" and "If you trusted God sufficiently you would be healed" create added torture in lives already drawn taut like a rubber band ready to break. To suffer and not to be understood is loneliness in any century and culture whether it be that of the ancient Job or of a Matthew Arnold living in the turmoil of the nineteenth-century Industrial Revolution or of twentieth-century visitors to a small village in Mexico escaping the feelings of future shock that have been the result of this century's rapid change and consequent confusion.

The depersonalization of American life has contributed greatly to our feelings of loneliness. We talk much about freedom to express ideas and acceptance of other people's rights, but we fight harder than most generations have fought to be understood—to *not* be alone. Family units are not close, and so no one hears as they did in previous decades. Friendships become mechanized into lists of how much I do for you and how much you do back for me. Sometimes on all sides it becomes just easier to pay a therapist to listen and hope he or she will at least understand. This has got to be the epitome of buying services that used to come in the name of friendship and love.

I held one child for an hour while she cried. Her parent later took her out of counseling because he had no *time* to take her to me. He didn't mind paying the money. He didn't intend to take the time to hold her and talk to her himself. But even time spent in having someone else understand her cut too deeply into his own, self-centered life-style. Yet ironically he, too, felt profoundly isolated on his little self-made psychological island where he neither extended himself for anyone nor was extended to by anyone else.

A caricature of what can occur in a fanatical depersonalization of human relationship is given to us in Colin Turnbull's description of the Ik, a fast-dying tribe in the mountains separating Uganda, the Sudan, and Kenya. Originally a hunting tribe cooperating in their work, the Ik were forced into becoming farmers by the creation of a national game reserve in Kenya. Drought and lack of technological knowledge about farming defeated them, and they have deteriorated into a tribe of fewer than two thousand, isolated from each other in an attempt to survive. Children are thrown out on their own at three. Old people are laughed at as they die. Family members take food from each other, even at the cost of causing death to a husband or a wife. There's no word for goodness left in their language, and there is no apparent desire for love or understanding. Loneliness is a way of life and as such is scarcely felt on a conscious level. Says Turnbull:

> There is no goodness left for the Ik, only a full stomach, and that only for those whose stomachs are already full. But if there is not goodness, stop to think, there is no badness, and if there is no love, neither is there any hate. Perhaps that, after all, is progress; but it is also emptiness.[4]

In relating the state of the Ik to the emotion of loneliness, Turnbull comments:

> Only Lokeléa *did* feel lonely, for although I detected signs, symptoms of loneliness, I think the others really felt nothing; though perhaps in reality that is the greatest loneliness of all. But Lokeléa felt deeply. I remember one night that really moved me with its beauty. There was a full moon and shortly after dark it rose above Meraniang and touched the

summit of Morungole, already silhouetted by a burning bush fire on the far side. Slowly and peacefully
that special silvery gleam spread down the side, leaving a shadow in the shape of the hills behind me.
Over the glimmering stretch of park, at the base of
Lotukoi, a tiny red glow told of a camp. I knew it
was Lomer, gathering honey out in that vast expanse,
and alone. I stayed awake a long time, and when I
went to sleep it seemed only a few minutes before I
heard Lokeléa. But it was half-past four in the morning, and the moonlight was gone and the beauty was
gone, and outside was nothing but blackness of night
and soul, cold and blustery. Lokeléa had awakened
to find his wife and children were already awake
with cold and hunger and were huddled over a fire.
He gave out a cry of despair that, being Lokeléa, he
turned to poetry and to song, asking how God could
allow such unhappiness and misery to those he had
let down from the sky; asking why he had retreated
beyond their reach, leaving them without hope. He
sang to himself and his wife and children for half an
hour, and then fell into a silence that was even more
bitter than the song.

For all around were others who also were cold and
hungry, but who had lost all trust in the world, lost
all love and all hope, who merely accepted life's bru-
tality and cruelty because it was empty of all else.
They had no love left that could be tortured and
compelled to express itself as grief, and no God to
sing to, for they were Ik.[5]

What struck Turnbull with violent force were the parallels
between the Ik and Western culture in the twentieth century.
Speaking of the Ik, he claims: "They are brought together by
self-interest alone, and the system takes care that such associa-
tion is of a temporary nature and cannot flourish into anything

as dysfunctional as affection or trust. Does that sound so very different from our own society . . . ?"[6]

Continues Turnbull regarding our own system: "What has become of the Western family? The very old and the very young are separated, but we dispose of them in homes for the aged or in day schools and summer camps instead of on the slopes of Meraniang. Marital relations are barely even fodder for comedians, and responsibility for health, education and welfare has been gladly abandoned to the state. . . . The individualism that is preached with a curious fanaticism, heightened by our ever growing emphasis on competitive sports, the more violent the better, and suicidal recreations, is of course at direct variance with our still proclaimed social ideals, but we ignore that, for we are already individuals at heart and society has become a game we play in our old age, to remind us of our childhood."[7]

The Ik present a caricature of isolation; but a society, like an individual, is in danger when its reality begins to approach caricature dimensions. For us, the caricature of the Ik is becoming reality. Isolation is no longer a caricature; it is reality. We talk about understanding, but we do not understand. We sing songs about love, but few of us really love. Worse still, few of us even know that our so-called love is merely an imitation of the real thing. We measure sex by how frequently we reach orgasm or get an erection rather than by how much we care to give of ourselves to that mate. We judge our children's success by educational accolades and material wealth. We must get and take and do our own thing—and then we wonder why we are lonely.

Loneliness is not the disease of our century. It is not a disease at all. It is the natural outcome of materialism, fast-pace living, buying of services, and extreme individualism. It is not pathology. It is emptiness as a result of collective pathology. Yet it is still possible for individuals within this society to experience something beyond loneliness.

* * *

Some friends were visiting and had brought with them their newest foster child, five-year-old Marc. It was getting late and Marc had fallen asleep on the sofa. Suddenly he woke up in sobs and came running to me. As I held him, I could see he felt as isolated in his own little world as any adult I had ever encountered. He was afraid to say what he felt, because the adult world might be angry and not understand. So I said it for him.

"Marc, did you have a nightmare?" I questioned.

"Yes"—then more sobs.

"Did you dream that you were back with your real parents?"

"Yes"—more sobs.

Finally I said, "Is that where you'd like to be right now?" His "Yes" broke the dam of resistance. He still hurt, but he was no longer alone, for he had been understood. He cried for a while, not out of panic, like before, but now more gently, more out of sadness. And then he fell asleep.

A young woman in her mid-twenties consulted me regarding her feelings of doubt about her relationship with God. Raised in a strict legalistic background, Peggy had kept her theological beliefs intact but had begun to differ vastly from her family in her beliefs about other issues of life, such as raising children, job preference, and friendship. Each time she came up with a new idea, someone in her family or church condemned her.

How could she send her child to nursery school while she worked? How could she allow her husband to trade off with her in the night when their child needed attention? Why did she want to work, anyway? These were just the start of multiple questions relating to her worth and relationship to God.

The pastor told her to become more involved in the church and she'd feel better. A Christian psychologist told her that it was society and he couldn't help her. A female therapist said that she couldn't relate to her problem but would be glad to be the sounding board for Peggy's anger. In short, Peggy was not understood, even by professionals. When she came to me, her anger was there prematurely, an anger that was coupled with a despairing kind of loneliness. We came to no immediate answers in that first session. Many solutions lay deeply entrenched in her improving her own defective view of herself. The more completely she learns to accept herself, the less she will feel lonely, for she will experience the capability to control her own life and thinking. On the other hand, in her discussions with me, there was visible relief in her face as she felt understood. As she rose to leave, she said tellingly: "I didn't know if anyone *could* understand me." She, too, for the moment, had risen beyond loneliness.

Dr. Rollo May magnificently expresses the therapeutic relationship in which one is understood and loneliness is dissolved at least for that moment. Says Dr. May:

> . . . it draws the other human being for a moment out of the loneliness of his individual existence and welcomes him into community with another soul. It is like inviting the traveler in from his snowy and chilly journey to warm himself for an hour before the fire on another's hearth. Such understanding, it is not too much to say, is the most objective form of love. That is why there is always a tendency on the part of the counselee to feel some love toward the counselor, this person "who understands me." There are few gifts that one person can give to another in this world as rich as understanding.[8]

What is true in psychotherapy, apart from the professional expertise, should be true in relationships, particularly those that claim the stamp of God's approval. In the New Testament, we read of the church portrayed as a body and that, as in the physical body, each part has value and contributes to the well-being of the whole. Furthermore, each part is valued and taken care of. Within the mystical body of Christ, the

church, one of the greatest ways we can help and value each
other is by genuine, gut-level understanding. If that understanding were operative, loneliness would not be as great a
problem to Christians, even within a society that generates
loneliness.

I was lonely the other day over a miscellaneous cluster of
problems that had to be solved in practical ways. My friend
who is not in business for herself said she'd pray. I said,
"Thanks," and went home still lonely. My other friend, also a
Christian, said, "Let's write the details down and, one by one,
decide on the best solution." Some of the solutions worked,
but even if they hadn't, my second friend understood, and
therefore before we even worked on the problem I felt less
loneliness.

I felt lonely one day back on that trip in Mexico. This time
my loneliness arose from my realization that my trip was
nearly over and I was afraid that when I got home I would
not feel rested enough to live up to all the commitments I had
made. Perhaps no vacation is long enough to really regenerate
one to the point where future work seems not only possible
but easy.

At any rate, this time I turned to my favorite writer, Amy
Carmichael. Poetically she wrote: "The trouble which
grieved the night has not floated off on the wings of the
morning. There has been a turning of the captivity and the
hard weather has passed . . . [but] there is a fact, a memory,
a possibility, that strikes up and faces us wherever we look.
That knot of painful circumstance is there. . . ."[9] I felt understood. She, too, knew what it was like to solve problems in
this world and yet to know their reoccurrence. Emerson was
accurate when he said that we find our own rejected thoughts
in great writings. What he was saying too was that often in
the reading of great writings we find ourselves understood. I
was understood that afternoon in Mexico and my loneliness
left. In my own way, I *had* found my bridge over troubled
waters. As one of my friends said later, half joking, "What-

ever you've been reading, I should carry it with me all the time."

Loneliness can be superficially alleviated in the multitude of activities in which Americans drown themselves. It can be anesthetized by drugs and alcohol. But unless more-substantial solutions are applied, the loneliness will remain and millions will continue to echo the words of one American woman:

> I can speed the day;
> A dozen chores dissolve my restlessness,
> A speck of dust,
> A spot of rust
> Can trap my loneliness.
>
> I cannot speed the night,
> Memories beat upon my window pane,
> I bathe in tears
> And count the years
> And watch my candle wane.
>
> Dianne Nevel

NOTES

1. *The Buried Life,* in *Poetry of the Victorian Period,* compiled by George Benjamin Woods and Jerome Hamilton Buckley (Chicago: Scott, Foresman and Company, 1955), p. 452.

2. Ibid.

3. Ibid., p. 453.

4. Colin M. Turnbull, *The Mountain People* (New York: Simon & Schuster, Inc., Pubs., 1972), p. 286.

5. Ibid., pp. 263–64.

6. Ibid., p. 290.

7. Ibid., p. 291.

8. Rollo May, *The Art of Counseling* (Nashville: Abingdon Press, 1967), p. 119.

9. Amy Carmichael, *Gold by Moonlight* (Fort Washington, Pa.: Christian Literature Crusade, 1970), p. 38.

2

Freeing Myself Through Aloneness

FIVE-YEAR-OLD Gerald had come to visit me with his parents. While everyone else was out swimming, Gerald and I talked. Stretched out on our stomachs across the bed in one of the rooms, we had a perfect view of the city at dusk. We watched planes with their flashing lights coming in to land at the airport a few miles away. But what Gerald enjoyed most were the occasional large trucks that came by on the street. Gerald loves trucks. And as he watched through the window he became relaxed and very talkative.

"I'm angry," he started.

"Why?" I returned, wondering what could have happened in such a seemingly tranquil scene to bring out feelings of anger.

"I'm angry because in the morning my sister comes into my room," Gerald replied. "I like to be alone when I wake up and she won't let me. Sometimes I just don't want to be around anyone."

A few minutes later the sound of several fire engines filled

the air. At first Gerald was thrilled. Then, as the sounds of the
sirens came closer and the dog next door began to howl with
an unearthly sound, Gerald's mood suddenly changed.

"Let's go where everyone else is," he said. "I feel too
alone."

What Gerald described about the feelings he has in the
morning was a desire for healthy aloneness. What he experienced after he heard the fire engines was painful loneliness.
Americans find aloneness difficult to handle. We must have
constant music and lots of people around us most of the time.
Yet we are lonely, although we are not alone much. In some
paradoxical way, because we cannot handle aloneness we become lonely even in a crowd.

Aloneness is the peaceful feeling I have when I leave my
office after a day of listening to the pain and problems of
others and find quietness in my home—and time to catch up
with myself. I can't do that in a crowd. Aloneness is expressed
in the sigh of relief uttered by a mother on that first day in
September when her children leave to start their year of
school and she is alone in a quiet house. Aloneness is peaceful
and private. Aloneness feels good.

Loneliness, on the other hand, is quite different. It is not
peaceful and does not feel good. It is, rather, a gnawing, aching emptiness that longs for someone who will come and fill it.
I asked a five-year-old what she thought loneliness was. She
answered: "Being quiet."

When I replied, "How does being quiet make you feel
lonely?" thinking that perhaps she really didn't know what the
word meant, she explained, "I'm quiet so that I won't make
anyone angry and then they won't yell at me." Isolation so
that people won't reject you certainly would be a definition of
loneliness and has been the theme of much writing for cen-
turies.

Anything that makes us feel not merely alone but alienated
or isolated from other human beings can be defined as pro-
ducing loneliness. In the Garden of Gethsemane, Christ was

lonely, partly because His three closest friends didn't understand His needs well enough to stay awake with Him. Conversely, guilt is a major factor in our human loneliness before God. Protestant legalism has unfortunately generated a large part of that feeling of alienating guilt. Says Paul Tournier in his book *Guilt and Grace:*

> We of the Reformed Church have great need today to recover the spirit which drew from Calvin the passionate cry: "To God alone be the glory!" These four centuries later we find ourselves in a somber period of history, when the Church contributes rather to the oppressing than to the liberating of souls. We were plunged into this situation at least by the beginning of the century, and this time it was the psychologists who raised the cry of alarm. And already theologians, Protestant as well as Catholic and Orthodox—struggle vigorously against a moralistic and activistic perversion of the Church.
>
> Yet I notice a larger proportion of people oppressed by this deviation amongst Protestants, even when their Church connection is slender, than amongst Catholics. The fulfillment of duty, the renunciation of all pleasure, good resolutions, the daily attempt to conquer one's faults, shame at one's instincts, the fear of being found fault with, judged, misunderstood—all this substituted for the zest of a love towards God. And in all these points one remains continually at fault, ever more hopeless, with defeat after defeat, constantly and increasingly fretted by guilt.
>
> This moralism itself multiplies defeats, because despair leads on to defeat by sapping the vital forces of the soul, and defeat leads to despair. It is precisely from this inexorable and vicious circle that God would deliver us by His unconditional forgiveness,

and it is tragic to see those who believe in Him and who seek to serve Him living lives crushed by these sinister coils even more than unbelievers, until they are no longer even able to love a God who seems to them so hard and so cruel.[1]

Not long ago, a young woman called me on a Sunday afternoon saying, "I am so tired of being with people who talk about God." Knowing her, as I do, to be a woman who seeks after God and who has identified herself with a large evangelical church in the area, I was surprised and not sure where she was coming from. And so I listened for something I had not perceived in order to hear what was really behind the otherwise contradictory words. She was lonely. That was one reason for her call to me. She was hurting deeply, as was evidenced by her labeling her message with the answering service as an emergency. Still she was shutting off her friends in her loneliness, thus preferring aloneness to friends who were making her feel lonely with regard to both God and man. For as she stumbled through her tearful explanation, what she really was saying was: "I'm trying to please God. But every time I think I'm okay my Christian friends talk about God in a way that makes me feel as though I'm sinning. Some say I should work, others that I should stay at home. Some consider my desire for relaxation and fun to be frivolous, others say I'm not a submissive wife."

The tears were a result of the frustration of not being acceptable to friends who had stricter beliefs than she did and consequently made her doubt God's love. Alienation from man and God through disapproval: that is loneliness!

To handle aloneness, without becoming lonely, is difficult in a culture that concentrates so much on togetherness. I remember one college professor of mine who said he believed that in the teaching of children it was better for the teacher not to know too much. "Togetherness" and the "we" feeling were his criteria for good education. If even studying and learning must be shared and cannot be done alone, we are indeed a sad, lonely generation.

Probably the most vital factor in learning to handle and enjoy aloneness is the level of a person's self-esteem. Liking oneself and one's own company makes aloneness pleasant and removes much of the loneliness we experience whether we are alone or in a crowd.

Self-esteem is the estimate that a person makes of his own worth. This involves two factors: an intellectual evaluation of one's worth and an emotional grasp and acceptance of that evaluation. Many people who consult me, for example, readily accept the fact with their intellect that they are intelligent people or that they are pretty. However, at the same time, they may make a statement like "But I don't feel like I'm intelligent (or pretty)." They *know* their worth with their heads, but they can't seem to *feel* it on a gut level. I suppose you could say that it is the difference between knowing that airplane travel is safe and feeling comfortable with flying. Many people know that air travel is safer statistically than freeway travel and yet will choose their chances on a freeway over those of flying. To know is not necessarily to feel.

As far as self-image is concerned, there are often two stages in therapy: first, getting a person to see who he really is, all his good points and areas that need change; then somehow helping him to *feel* that positive self-image instead of the previous, distorted idea of himself that he may have been carrying around all his life.

Such a transition takes time. Little children learn early to perceive who they are from those who are the closest, and thus the most formative, influence in their lives. A six-year-old said to me, "I'm no good. I can't do anything well." Already she was lonely. She didn't like herself and felt no one else could either. And in her world they didn't. Her parents were too strung out on drugs to know that she existed, and her grandparents were too busy to become involved. They treated her as though she were a nuisance, someone they could do without. And in her six-year-old head, that meant she had no worth. When this six-year-old is sixteen, she may be able to *see* logically that she is okay and that it was her childhood world that was messed up. But even at that there will be the scars, of all those years of believing that she was no good, that will need to be overcome. She will have to learn by a similar method of repetition and relationships, probably with a counselor, that she really is okay. Then the low self-esteem can be reversed to high self-esteem.

In some people, however, their self-image is at least partially accurate but low because they must make changes in their lives if they are to like themselves. On a somewhat simplistic level, the student who hates himself for not studying should study if he wants to improve his feelings about himself.

On a slightly more complicated level, it is very difficult for me to say no to anyone who makes a request of me. In the past, that has often led to bad feelings about myself, because when I made commitments I had no time to fulfill, then other commitments I needed to fulfill became harder to meet. Sometimes I have helped a friend but missed an hour with a patient. Or at times I have been overtired in writing because I cooked dinner for someone who should not have been a first priority in my life at that time. As I prayed and thought and talked out my priorities and acted upon them, my life had order and my self-esteem went up. For no one can have a good self-image whose life is not under her or his control timewise.

Yet this kind of growth involves change. And change is new. And new is scary. For me it was scary to tell people no. I felt stronger about myself but nervous about misunderstanding and rejection on the part of others. Yet growth and change and increased self-esteem are essential to the problem of loneliness. If I like myself and feel comfortable about myself, I will enjoy times of aloneness. And when I'm in a crowd I still will feel comfortable with myself and therefore will not feel lonely.

There are multitudes of Biblical examples that back up not only the validity of good self-esteem but its relationship to the subject of loneliness. When Joseph was trapped and sold into Egypt as a slave because of his brothers' jealousy, he would never have made it if he had been groveling around talking about how bad he was. He never denied the truth of his father's favoritism, nor did he flaunt it. He was neither self-abnegating nor arrogant. He was honest. He trusted the God-given wisdom of his dreams and therefore won favor with the king. He would not succumb to the wiles of a woman who had the potential to destroy him, even though it caused him to be in great disfavor for a while. Here was a man who liked himself and as a result trusted God. He didn't waste his time thinking that God couldn't possibly use him or that he was being punished for being his father's favorite. And because he was self-confident, he could trust God even more and eventually saved the lives of those same brothers who had sought to destroy him.

Likewise, Deborah, an Old Testament prophetess and judge, had a self-confidence that enabled her to be more usable by God. When Barak needed her assistance in going to battle, she agreed to go on the condition that he realize that when they won, she, a woman, would receive the credit. Barak agreed, Deborah fought, and they won.

In the New Testament, the disciples got into trouble when they got insecure about their worth and fought over who would be first in heaven. Peter failed when he was so insecure about himself that he let a maid intimidate him into denying Christ. Later a more confident Peter actually laid down his life for Jesus Christ.

Looking back over the lives of these people, there is often a correlation between their level of confidence and their loneliness. Joseph was consistently self-confident. It is also repeatedly stated that God was with him in a very special way. And

whether he was with his brothers, or unjustly accused of rape
and thus in prison, or a leader in Egypt with only the king as
his single superior, Joseph was at peace within himself. He
encouraged others and made the best of each situation.

It is impossible to draw a neat line between self-acceptance
and the working of God in our lives, but as the disciples grew
emotionally and spiritually, they too were able to endure rejection, imprisonment, and a host of difficulties that engender
loneliness. For self-respect does diminish lonely feelings.

It is interesting to note that when Jonah's self-image was
down at an extreme low, partly due to fatigue, he even felt
threatened by God's graciousness to the town of Nineveh,
which was, after all, the town to which he had been sent in
order that the citizens might be helped. When he could have
been rejoicing with God and man over his success in Nineveh,
he sat in isolation and depression, all alone and lonely, and
prayed to die. His was not the refreshing, restoring aloneness
that can follow battle. His was a fatigued, self-hating loneliness that was not even responsive at that time to the presence
of God Himself, much less to the positive influence of any
human being. For, very often, other people do help us to handle or avoid feelings of loneliness.

Just as self-esteem is interrelated with loneliness, so relationships with other people are vital to both a good self-image
and the handling and reducing of feelings of loneliness. In a
friendship, each gives and takes from the other. That give-
and-take is not always equal, for under particular stress the
person under stress will generally take more than he gives. In
a good friendship, however, there is a flow of give-and-take
and also a sense of freedom, not ownership. There is a quality
of trust that is the outgrowth of time and testing. For friendship, like marriage, does not arrive in full bloom. It must grow
and be cultivated.

A good friendship involves a process of declarations, each
stating where he is at a given time. For example, in order to
have this day to write I had to make several declarations to

several people. I explained to a friend that I would not be able to talk to her until later or it would break my train of thought. I asked, nicely, someone else not to call until this afternoon for the same reason. In order to be rested today, I didn't stay up late with company last night. All I had to say was that I was planning to go to bed early and fortunately my guest understood. Sometimes people don't understand. But in a good friendship each person should be able to state what he must do and be. He does not have the right to ask the other person to change for him, but he himself can state what he will and will not do. A friendship that cannot tolerate this honesty may not be worth having and is not the kind of relationship that militates against loneliness.

For friendship doesn't automatically make people less lonely. Only a good friendship does that. A lady went to lunch with three friends. In the course of the conversation, each of the other three women discussed their recent exotic vacations. Quietly the other lady listened. Feeling increasingly threatened, she finally told a story about a vacation her distant cousin had recently taken, and related it as if it were her own. Intrigued, her friends listened and were impressed. When the lady saw me next in my office, she said: "I couldn't let them know I was fifty-two, out of work, friendless, and lonely." Needless to say, her relationship with these three women does nothing to ameliorate her loneliness; it just increases that feeling.

In contrast, a few weeks ago, after a period of heavy stress in my life, a friend and I went out to eat. She knew that I was overtired and also that I needed to talk. We did all the things that usually help me. We went to a quiet restaurant overlooking the beach, and she listened to me for a while. Sometimes we were just silent, for she can tolerate that, too. Often she made such supportive statements as: "It's been rough, but it's over and that should be a relief." Not profound! No! But comforting, and that's what I wanted that Saturday night. Then we walked out by a path that overlooked the waves. Somehow, watching the ocean sweep over the green, mossy rocks and then recede back into itself again was very quieting and inspiring. Something in this world seemed permanent and secure again. In my tiredness and frustration I never felt that awful, gnawing loneliness. Rather, aloneness once again became a chance to rest, to just be, and to refurbish my energies for the work I had to do.

For, in some intricate, interwoven way, a good self-image, nourished by good relationships, enables a person to develop the potential we all have to cope with aloneness and to use aloneness to alleviate loneliness. For, once we have enough sense of enjoyment of our own being, our own company, we have taken a major step against loneliness.

Yet aloneness is not something we automatically handle. It must be cultivated. And in our society, where we avoid being alone, we are not used to having a positive attitude toward it. As has been said before, without the sense of well-being that comes from a reasonably good self-image and positive feedback from friends, aloneness will not usually be a tolerable state. However, once a person accepts himself and has some good relationships, a healthy enjoyment of aloneness can be cultivated which will be a strong defense against loneliness.

For each of us aloneness is a unique, singular experience. We do it differently from each other. For me, I have learned to enjoy aloneness before I go to bed. I try to go to bed earlier than I expect to sleep. Then I read. I go with my mood—anything from magazines to the fantasy of the *Chronicles of Narnia* to something thought-provoking like the writings of Paul Tournier or Viktor Frankl. When I want total comfort, I read the Psalms or something from Amy Carmichael. I know my needs and I follow them. Talking—and I love to talk!—would be an intrusion on this quiet time that I have with myself.

Other, similar times of aloneness for me are a walk on the beach, especially with my dog Thackeray, or listening to Bach with the lights turned down and a few candles burning, or even a hot bubble bath with candlelight and a magazine.

Trivial? Yes! Simplistic? True! But this for me is constructive aloneness and it is the opposite of loneliness. For sometimes in our busyness we need to learn to be alone, to focus on our thoughts, to crystallize what we really want in life, to know who we are when no one else is around.

For some, aloneness could be experienced positively in a sport or on a hill or riding a motorcycle across a desert.

Anne Morrow Lindbergh eloquently expresses her feelings about aloneness as it relates to her individual personality:

> For a full day and two nights I have been alone. I lay on the beach under the stars at night alone. I made my breakfast alone. Alone I watched the gulls at the end of the pier, dip and wheel and dive for the scraps I threw them. A morning's work at my desk, and then, a late picnic lunch alone on the beach. And it seemed to me, separated from my own species, that I was nearer to others: the shy willet, nesting in the ragged tide-wash behind me; the sandpiper, running in little unfrightened steps down the shining beach rim ahead of me; slowly flapping pelicans over my head, coasting down wind; the old gull, hunched up, grouchy, surveying the horizon. I felt a kind of impersonal kinship with them and a joy in that kinship. Beauty of earth and sea and air meant more to me. I was in harmony with it, melted into the universe, lost in it, as one is lost in a canticle of praise, swelling from an unknown crowd in a cathedral. "Praise ye the Lord, all ye fishes of the sea—all ye birds of the air—all ye children of men—Praise ye the Lord!"
>
> Yes, I felt closer to my fellow men too, even in my solitude. For it is not physical solitude that actually separates one from other men, not physical isolation, but spiritual isolation. It is not the desert island nor the stony wilderness that cuts you from the people

you love. It is the wilderness in the mind, the desert
wastes in the heart through which one wanders lost
and a stranger. When one is a stranger to oneself
then one is estranged from others too. If one is out of
touch with oneself, then one cannot touch others.
How often in a large city, shaking hands with my
friends, I have felt the wilderness stretching between
us. Both of us were wandering in arid wastes, having
lost the springs that nourished us—or having found
them dry. Only when one is connected to one's own
core is one connected to others, I am beginning to
discover. And, for me, the core, the inner spring, can
best be refound through solitude.[2]

Then adds Mrs. Lindbergh:

Solitude, says the moon shell. Every person, especially every woman, should be alone sometime during the year, some part of each week, and each day.
How revolutionary that sounds and how impossible
of attainment. To many women such a program
seems quite out of reach. They have no extra income
to spend on a vacation for themselves; no time left
over from the weekly drudgery of housework for a
day off; no energy after the daily cooking, cleaning
and washing for even an hour of creative solitude.

Is this then only an economic problem? I do not
think so. Every paid worker, no matter where in the
economic scale, expects a day off a week and a vacation a year. By and large, mothers and housewives
are the only workers who do not have regular time
off. They are the great vacationless class. They rarely
even complain of their lack, apparently not considering occasional time to themselves as a justifiable
need.

Herein lies one key to the problem. If women were

convinced that a day off or an hour of solitude was a
reasonable ambition, they would find a way of at-
taining it. As it is, they feel so unjustified in their
demand that they rarely make the attempt. One has
only to look at those women who actually have the
economic means or the time and energy for solitude
yet do not use it, to realize that the problem is not
solely economic. It is more a question of inner con-
victions than of outer pressures, though, of course,
the outer pressures are there and make it more
difficult. As far as the search for solitude is concerned, we live in a negative atmosphere as invisible,
as all-pervasive, and as enervating as high humidity
on an August afternoon. The world today does not
understand, in either man or woman, the need to be
alone.[3]

Indeed we all need to learn to enjoy aloneness in our own
way so that in turn we can handle not only loneliness better
but, indeed, our whole lives.

I first met five-year-old Gerald, who was referred to as this
chapter started, when he was two. He was in a foster home
due to illness in the family and used to sit silently in his crib,
at times for hours, sucking his thumb and saying nothing. His
was not healthy aloneness. It was the loneliness of a child lost
and bewildered in a world that was strange and frightening.
Gerald has learned a little to enjoy aloneness, and he is not as
lonely as he used to be. He likes his waking hours to be undis-
turbed. And when he comes to my house he loves to lie on my
bed and watch the lights outside.

Yet the other evening he crawled into my lap and asked:
"Will I ever have to leave my parents again?" There was a
frightened look on his face and a terror of once again feeling
lonely. "No," I answered. "You will stay with them until you
grow up." Impulsively Gerald flung his arms around my neck
and whispered: "I love you. You make me feel good."

What Gerald was really saying was: "I'm lonely, but you make me feel less lonely." He's still in that transition between being solely dependent on relationships to ameliorate loneliness, trying increasingly to like himself better, and occasionally enjoying aloneness—and feeling stronger and less lonely with each positive experience.

In a sense, we are all a little like Gerald. Here we are in this great big world. We aren't five, so we act our age. But we fear the loss of our supports whether they be people or things. And while we know that no one else can get inside our skin and be us and understand us, sometimes we wish they could. Yet we, too, have our flashes of really enjoying being alone. And it is in the cultivation of those "flashes" that we can find an important weapon against loneliness. For if Norman Cousins was correct when he stated that "All man's history is an endeavor to shatter his loneliness,"[4] it is also true that it can be shattered and that aloneness can be one tool in that endeavor.

NOTES

1. Paul Tournier, *Guilt and Grace* (New York: Harper & Row, Publishers, 1962), pp. 196–97.

2. Anne Morrow Lindbergh, *Gift from the Sea* (New York: The New American Library, 1961), pp. 42–44.

3. Ibid., pp. 47–49.

4. Norman Cousins, "Modern Man Is Obsolete" (New York: Viking Press, 1945), p. 13.

3

Living Beyond Loneliness

BY THE TIME I was seven, we were well into polio epidemics without the benefit of a polio vaccine. Years later, after the torture of long hot summers when my friends did get polio and one even died, Jonas Salk seemed a great hero to me when he developed that first vaccine. It ended those fearful summer days when public pools and crowded places were spots to be avoided.

But, at the age of seven, polio was a real threat to me, which parental anxiety constantly brought to my awareness by the limitations imposed on my life. The Lindbergh kidnaping case was also a fresh memory in my parents' minds. And so I lived with constant admonitions, this time about strangers and cars.

In my childish mind, I had comprehended that, as a Christian, I could certainly refer to God for help in these matters. But, Protestant as I was, just asking Him didn't seem enough. Pure grace alone seemed a little too scary to trust. And so I bargained with God. I would read so many chapters in the Bible a day for protection from polio and kidnapers. I doubt that such negotiating maneuvers did much to move the Deity, but psychologically it gave me a sense of security.

Theologically I knew the tenets of evangelical Christianity and was committed to them regarding the salvation of my soul. But something in me was starting which I believe is basic to every person's being, a personal quest for truth or for greater reassurance about the truth he already has.

In a way, at seven I was a cross between an evangelical Christian (salvation by grace), a Roman Catholic (my attempts at a manipulation of God by works), and even one of those tortured nineteenth-century poets who proclaimed, at times blasphemously, to God their independence of Him or at least of established dogmas. I wasn't exactly shouting with Henley,

> I am the master of my fate:
> I am the captain of my soul.

Yet in my own childish way I was searching out my own truth, making sure that I did something myself about my personal safety. I couldn't believe that faith and prayer were enough. Now I know how silly my negotiations with almighty God were, but I do respect them as the evidence of a beginning of a search within my soul to find out about God, rather than only to parrot what I had been taught. For what comes out of such a search becomes more deeply than ever a part of a person's being.

Yet such searching is painfully lonely. At seven I was lonely during those hours in my bedroom, reading my chapters, asking God if this was truly enough.

Nor does such a quest for valid, concrete meaning in this world stop in childhood or even after one becomes an evangelical Christian.

Knowing Jesus Christ in a personal way, not as the Deist's remote God (who wound up this earth like a top, set it in motion, and left), but knowing Him as a personal God daily involved in one's life, answers many basic questions of meaning. But not all. For there are various kinds of meaning in life not necessarily directly related to God, such as the ministrations of a skilled surgeon. And more important, one must apply specifically in one's life the meaning that one does find in God. Thus, within the scope of Christian belief there can be the loneliness of a search for certain aspects of meaning as well as the filling up of what Frankl calls the "existential vacuum."

Even within the Christian scope, applying meaning to one's life can bring comfort. We in the evangelical Protestant world loudly disclaim a Pope. Yet we have many popes instead of one. Great nationally known spiritual leaders carry weight. We feel better if we agree with them, or worse if we do not. And we have our own personal popes. They are harder to resist, because we know them, love them, and are vulnerable to them. When I was in my twenties, I associated with a group of students and college professors who were truly godly people and who consequently enriched my life spiritually. Yet, the unspoken requirement for acceptance was agreement with their views of God. We did not talk about the deity of Christ or the doctrines of the Trinity, for which we might well lay down our lives. But details much more open to debate were the issues. And frankly, had we been debating a major theological point, I would still have expected more love and decency than they showed toward people who disagreed with them.

As I began a more independent thought process, I started to ask questions. It was the beginning of a final break in our relationship. The peak came one afternoon when I asked the question:

"What if a man came to your house with a hatchet, determined to kill your wife? She is hiding under the bed in the bedroom. The man asks the question: 'Is your wife home, where can I find her?' What would your answer be?" I concluded.

"I could not lie," the student leader, a faculty member of the university, replied. "The Bible says not to lie so I couldn't, not even to save a life."

A little nonplussed and certainly not wishing to dispute the validity of the Scriptures, I asked a further series of questions:

"Do you own a car?"

"Yes," he replied.

"Did you buy it with cash or credit?" I continued.

"Credit," he answered. Adding, "Nobody buys with cash these days."

"How do you deal with the Biblical command to 'Owe no man anything'?" I concluded.

Silence prevailed. There were no consistent answers. I thought of Corrie Ten Boom's father hiding Jews and concealing that fact from the Nazis. What if my friend had been in Holland or Germany during that period in history?

It was one of those times when you know that you have not only lost an argument but a friend as well. For, in their minds, unless I took their point of view on this, I no longer had a proper relationship with God and thus with them. Obviously, I had lost some respect for their opinion. I had lost my own personal popes, and I felt lonely.

There is a deep loneliness in seeking truth and meaning in "this" world when you encounter such a circumstance. It has always been a little lonely to be a Christian in a world that does not always embrace the teachings of Christ. But to be lonely within a group of believers is to be lonely at a peak of intensity. Yet how often Christ must have felt such loneliness! He ate with sinners and was criticized. He did good deeds on the Sabbath and was accused of breaking the law. He turned over tables of money in the Temple. And in the Garden of Gethsemane, He rebuked His own disciples when Peter tried to rescue Him in a mistaken notion of what was right.

Jesus Christ knew the loneliness of misunderstanding. Once again we need to remember that He begged His three closest friends to stay awake while He prayed in the garden. He needed them. And He was lonely without them.

As we each search for application of the meaningfulness of Jesus Christ in our own lives, we will at times differ from each other. That need not be such a lonely experience if we offer each other mutual support if not complete understanding and agreement. It is when we alienate others in our inflexibility, or are alienated from others, that the loneliness sets in. Such alienation is the opposite of all the teachings and the very gut-level feeling that Christ taught.

For, rather than contributing to loneliness, Christian teaching fills in the gap of emptiness with which man seems to have been created. An emptiness that, according to Augustine, can be filled only by God.

It has been said by some that those who live in the light of eternity's values are those so oppressed on this earth that they only look forward to heaven. However, with a clearer ring of reality, I remember a statement once made by a sixteen-year-old student of mine:

"Why should I feel that life is meaningful?" he asked. "If I go on the way I am, I'll be just like my father. He has a nice house, two cars, a wife and kids. Oh, yes, and a prestigious job with regular raises and promotions. Then some day he'll die and leave it all to his kids. Is he happy? No! Sad? No! He makes it. But that's not good enough for me."

In our century perhaps no single human being has commented so meaningfully on the need for a purpose in life as has Dr. Viktor Frankl. While Frankl's ideas are not couched in a religious context, they are easily compatible with Christian thinking.

To the man who says, "Life has nothing else to offer me," Frankl replies, "But you still owe something *to* life."

When he was interned in a concentration camp, Frankl offered this one basic idea to those around him: that he who knows the *why* of his existence can endure any *how*.

Perhaps a peak of Frankl's declaration of meaning is expressed best by him at the end of his book *The Will to Meaning.*

In searching for his own meaning, Frankl says:

> I myself went through this purgatory when I found myself in a concentration camp and lost the manuscript of the first version of my first book. Later, when my own death seemed imminent, I asked myself what my life had been for. Nothing was left which would survive me. No child of my own. Not even a spiritual child such as the manuscript. But after wrestling with my despair for hours, shivering from typhus fever, I finally asked myself what sort of meaning could depend on whether or not a manuscript is printed. I would not give a damn for it. But if there is meaning, it is unconditional meaning, and neither suffering nor dying can detract from it.
>
> . . . In the past nothing is irrecoverably lost but everything is irrevocably stored. People see only the stubble field of transitoriness but overlook the full granaries of the past in which they have delivered and deposited, in which they have saved, their harvest.
>
> But what about those miserable creatures whose granaries are empty, as it were, what about the senile men, the sterile women, and those artists and scientists whose desks and drawers are empty rather than full of manuscripts? What about them? The unconditional faith in an unconditional meaning may turn the complete failure into a heroic triumph. That this is possible has not only been demonstrated by many a patient in our days but also by a peasant who lived in Biblical times, somewhere in Palestine. His were granaries in the literal sense. And they were literally empty. And yet, out of an unconditional trust in ulti-

mate meaning, and an unconditional faith in ultimate being, Habakkuk chanted his triumphant hymn:

"Although the fig tree shall not blossom, neither shall fruit be in the vines; the labor of the olive shall fail, and the fields shall yield no meat; the flock shall be cut off from the fold, and there shall be no herd in the stalls: Yet I will rejoice in the Lord, I will joy in the God of my salvation."[1]

"The unconditional faith in an unconditional meaning may turn the complete failure into a heroic triumph." This also is the essence of a Christian's meaning in life, the filling up of Frankl's "existential vacuum."

Contrary especially to current Christian thinking, success is not superficial. It is not always measurable in wealth or numbers. If it were, our hold on meaning would be tenuous indeed. Failure is a lonely experience, but failure indeed depends in a basic way upon one's definition of failure and success. Sometimes we feel we fail when we most succeed and we succeed when we feel that we have failed.

Robert Browning expresses the same thought as Frankl on unconditional meaning; only, he wrote his words in the 1860s and expressed his thoughts in poetic form. In referring to God as the Potter and man as the clay, Browning says:

> Earth changes, but thy soul and God stand sure:
>   What entered into thee,
>   *That* was, is, and shall be:
> Time's wheel runs back or stops: Potter and clay endure.[2]

In Browning's mind, not only is meaning enduring, but he defines success in succinct, meaningful language:

>   All I could never be,
>   All, men ignored in me,
> This, I was worth to God, whose wheel the pitcher shaped.[3]

What Browning is really saying in the nineteenth century and Frankl in the twentieth is that success consists first of all in being, and thus meaning too resides in who we are. Who am I when no one sees me? Who does my Creator know me to be? What are my motives?

For me, I ask the questions: Why do I write? Why do I help people? Why do I say yes or no? Who am I in my hidden parts? For who I am there gives me my meaning, or my lack of meaning.

However, to find meaning in who we are requires that we recognize those qualities within ourselves that give our individual lives meaning. The fact that we have been made in God's image and for fellowship with Him automatically gives our lives meaning. Yet it is important to follow through on specific application of these facts.

A young man frantically called me on the phone. It was a Saturday night, and he was completely coming apart emotionally. His first thought had been to call the paramedics. Then a friend had urged him to call me. Jim came to me for a number of months following that phone call. He had some severe physical-emotional problems, but what always impressed me was his attitude. He was a kind person, and even though he suffered greatly he never took his anger out on others. He had a kind of character and toughness that one respects.

Yet, ironically, with all this inner strength, one of Jim's greatest problems lay in his inability to see that strength. For a long time he repeatedly denigrated himself for even having emotional problems. Intellectually, he could see that he was doing a good job of not inflicting his problems on other people. Yet it took months for him to feel the good of that on a gut level. When he did, his self-esteem rose tremendously and he saw the meaning in his life that existed *because* of the way he had handled his suffering. The loneliness of a meaningless existence was exchanged for the fulfillment found in meaning.

Perhaps never was Viktor Frankl quite so successful personally as when he became heroic in the truest sense of that word

as a prisoner in the Nazi camps. Never is our worth greater
than when we become all that we were meant to be, even
while enduring the crucible of suffering.

Yet, for most of us, suffering is not a constant, permanent
state. While pain is interspersed throughout our lives, most of
us still have a more neutral span of time and energy throughout our lives, which becomes very lonely indeed unless it is
focused on a task. Our life tasks arise out of *who* we are, and
for the Christian that task is ultimately aimed at pleasing our
Taskmaster. It is at this point that we must move from general
theological knowledge to concrete action.

A pastor friend of mine preaches the love of God from the
pulpit. But his task would still leave him feeling empty if he
stopped there. And he doesn't. In many concrete ways he
shows that love of God which he has preached. He translates
his theology of God's love to the very practical issue of a hospital room or a counseling session.

We wonder why as Christians we have meaning and yet
don't *feel* that meaning. We wonder at our emptiness. Yet, all
the time, we are hugging our theology to ourselves, forgetting
or ignoring the fact that God demands specific tasks from
each of us that should be the outgrowth of that theology.

An evangelist who traveled from city to city preaching at
various churches became involved in a particularly long series
of preaching tours. Toward the end of the second week, his
fourteen-year-old son called.

"Dad, I need you. Can you please come home?" the boy
pleaded with tears.

The man had rarely heard his son cry. Yet, without even
further questioning, the man replied, curtly: "Don't bother
me when you know I'm busy. I'll talk to you in a couple of
weeks."

They never talked. Three hours later, the boy was dead, an
apparent suicide from an overdose.

Life task? Meaning? With all of his busyness the man had
little of either. Oh, he was in so-called Christian work all of

his life, but so much of it was just busyness. Power was sought for the sake of power, not as a means toward a God-directed end. He even escaped from responsibilities through excessive travel. He never really sought for or found a specific life task that in itself was real and genuine enough to give him meaning. He did a lot of things in the name of God, and inadvertently some of his activities helped the world. But his priorities and focus were so blurred and his motivation so faulty that his "existential vacuum" was never filled up. Having failed in the truest Browning sense of that word, he died alone in alcoholism.

It is not good enough just to be a Christian—unless, of course, all one is interested in is a passport to heaven. It's not good enough just to be busy, for busyness in itself can be the epitome of emptiness. For to experience meaning in this world requires a careful consideration of one's specific life goals. For the Christian, such a consideration involves a deep, personal evaluation of the will of God.

In our own individual encounters with God, we each are led by different means. A single most formative influence on the early shaping of my life goals came from reading the works of the British missionary to India Amy Carmichael.

In *Kohila,* Amy Carmichael says:

All that troubles is only for a moment. Nothing is important but that which is eternal.[4]

Later in the same book, she expands that thought a little:

For the eternal substance of a thing never lies in the thing itself, but in the quality of our reaction towards it. If in hard times we are kept from resentment, held in silence and filled with inward sweetness, that is what matters. The event that distressed us will pass from memory as a wind that passes and is gone. But what we were while the wind was blowing upon us has eternal consequences.

And watch for the comforts of God. When Earl Jellicoe was being misunderstood by the nation he served so faithfully, a letter came to him from King George, whose keen sea-sense had penetrated the mist which had bemused the general public. His letter heartened the Fleet. What did anything matter now? "Their King knew."[5]

The impact of eternity on our life tasks and that stabilizing line, "Their King knew," have held my focus, or helped me refocus, many times. For when the events of my life become channeled within the context of these two concepts, my life becomes meaningful and there is no existential void.

It is amazing, for example, how trivia drop off and become exposed as just that—trivia—when I consider their worth in the light of fifty years from now. Petty criticism becomes less traumatic if in truth my King, my Taskmaster, my God knows and understands what I am doing. Life becomes simplified down to its essentials. And those essentials become meaningful to my existence.

For each person, the search for meaning must be his own private quest. For even within the Christian scope, while we have salvation in common, we have uniqueness before God in our specific life tasks.

A large number of people I meet find no meaning in their jobs, and stifle their urges for meaning with an endless round of activities designed to bury their desire for meaning, rather than to fulfill it.

Christianity offers meaning. But even here, meaning must be discovered, made concrete, made personal. To come so far as to be a Christian and then to miss the fullness of meaning involved is indeed loneliness. To find that meaning is truly to be beyond loneliness.

NOTES

1. Viktor E. Frankl, *The Will to Meaning* (New York: The New American Library, Inc., 1969), pp. 156–57.

2. *Rabbi Ben Ezra*, verse xxvii, in *Poems of Robert Browning*, ed. Donald Smalley (Boston: Houghton Mifflin Company, 1956), p. 286.

3. Ibid., verse xxv.

4. Amy Carmichael, *Kohila* (Fort Washington, Pa.: Christian Literature Crusade, n.d.), p. 131.

5. Ibid., p. 135.

4 ⚜

Controlling Loneliness Through Structure

"OUR TRIP REALLY helped me," my friend commented. "It was just what I needed to relax and begin another year at my job." I agreed. Rarely had I slept so well and enjoyed a day's activities so much as on our ten-day vacation in Mexico. The remoteness of the little village had made me feel far away from pressure and demands. The ocean and the warmth of the sun had had their usual restorative effects. The people had been kind, the food unusually good, and I had indulged to the hilt my love of roaming about in small, out-of-the-way stores. Yet, for me, there had still been something lacking. All through the week I had experienced a slight tightness and a feeling of irritation, which I found impossible to shake off. I didn't understand why, and since my companions seemed to be enjoying themselves, I felt a little confused and lonely.

After my friend's comment, suddenly I knew the answer. She has a quieter job than I do, with fewer emotional demands. I am surrounded by people with needs, and my job as a therapist is to help these people in the filling of those needs. I love my work, but for me a vacation is not found in being confronted with people who talk about problems or even with too heavily philosophical discussions. My friend, on the other hand, finds that a fairly deep involvement with people is a healthy change from office routine.

For some reason, on this trip we constantly seemed to encounter people with needs, lonely people, people who desperately wanted to talk. For me that part had been tiring, while for my friend it had been a refreshing change.

Similarly, when I taught school I did not enjoy television shows that revolved around classroom incidents. Now I don't like most psychological-type TV shows. Watching them is too much like work. I can't take them lightly; I become intensely serious.

Commonality of interest and enjoyment brings feelings of comradeship and fellowship. When others enjoy something and we don't, we feel isolated and thus lonely. On my vacation that year, I had enjoyed the solitary walks along the beach. I could relate to quiet chats with one or two friends. But all of the outgoing involvement with total strangers who often discussed their problems left me drained. I couldn't even get wholeheartedly into the conversations, and so I felt left out on the fringes, and lonely. Maybe when we say we feel lonely in a crowd we are just with the wrong crowd for us at that time in our lives.

Knowing who we are, our needs, our personalities, our usual routine, even our family background, can help us structure our lives in an attempt to minimize loneliness. I use the word minimize guardedly, for we make a mistake and set ourselves up for failure when we expect to eradicate unpleasant feelings. Loneliness, like boredom, depression, terror, anxiety, love, joy, and hope, is a feeling that only insanity can completely eradicate. The psychotic who has no sense of self may truly feel nothing. But the price of nonbeing is high. For the rest of us, loneliness is an inevitable, painful part of life, but it *can* be minimized and controlled. With that goal in mind we can expect success, and one tool toward achieving our end is structuring our lives.

Those human beings in history who have achieved consistent greatness have usually had a very firm structure in their lives.

In his eightieth year, John Wesley wrote in his journal:

> I set out for Inverness [a town in Scotland]. . . . To ease the horses, we walked forward from Nairn, ordering Richard to follow us, as soon as they were fed; he did so, but then there were two roads. So, as we took one, and he the other, we walked about twelve miles and a half of the way, through heavy rain. . . . But, blessed be God, I was no more tired than when I set out from Nairn.[1]

Then he preached!

On his eighty-fifth birthday, Wesley described the structure that had brought him thus far with, as he put it, a realization of "how little have I suffered yet by 'the rush of numerous years.'"

> To what cause can I impute this, that I am as I am? First, doubtless, to the power of God, fitting me for the work to which I am called, as long as He pleases to continue me therein; and, next, subordinately to this, to the prayers of His children. May we not impute it as inferior means,
>
> 1. To my constant exercise and changes of air?
> 2. To my never having lost a night's sleep, sick or well, at land or at sea, since I was born?
> 3. To my having slept at command so that whenever I feel myself almost worn out I call it and it comes, day or night?

4. To my having constantly, for about sixty years, risen at four in the morning?

5. To my constant preaching at five in the morning, for about fifty years?

6. To my having had so little pain in my life; and so little sorrow, or anxious care?[2]

Perhaps some of Wesley's points are difficult for us to relate to, but going back even to the description of his early childhood upbringing, all the way through his life there was structure. And that structure made the pieces of his life fit together no matter what the stress. There was an organized, driving force about his life that militated against loneliness.

Let me contemporize this point a little: An elderly woman who had just lost her husband returned to her empty house. The temptations were many: move away, sit home and mourn, sleep late and eat little, avoid friends, question God. Yet somehow on a gut level she knew that the normal structure of her life must continue if she was to survive. She rose at her usual hour, cooked company meals when she felt up to it, continued to do the gardening and continued some redecorating on the house. She taught art, as she had before, and continued to exhibit her paintings. Change is new, and new is scary and lonely. The change of no husband and of living alone had been quite enough to make her feel lonely. And at times that loneliness became acute. But because the basic structure of her life did not change, that security ameliorated some of the loneliness, for it ensured that much was still familiar.

But, as we have seen, structure relates to more than just time management. A recently divorced lady told me that she fears living alone, yet she wants her own, private place. Her compromise? She has bought a town house where she is closely surrounded by people and yet her house is a separate entity and her own domain. She is alone and not lonely. She maintains her privacy and yet has not sacrificed a sense of physical closeness to other human beings.

The type of work one does also should determine the structure of one's life. When I taught school, for example, I was with groups of people all day and had many social contacts with other teachers. At night my relaxation was TV or a quiet dinner with a friend. Now that I am a writer and counselor my needs are different. Because of the intensity of the day, I need an hour or two to be alone. And that aloneness no longer feels lonely. It feels good. It is a time to be, to catch up with myself, my thinking, who I am. I seem to spend much more time contemplatively watching the waves of the ocean beating against the sandy shore. Aloneness does not frighten me as it once did. I also need a more complete social life, since there is none in my job. I require almost two extremes, time to be alone and then people who do not make demands emotionally.

Two of my friends who are secretaries have entirely different needs. After work they like to do something exciting and energetic. This year they enjoyed the Christmas mobs in the department stores, whereas I avoided the confusion by shopping early.

To put it simply, what we do all day becomes what we avoid in recreation: One person's work becomes another person's recreation. I do some counseling with small children in which I use games; therefore, party games are boring to me. I cannot find recreation in the playing of games. But I do not feel lonely or left out when I don't fit into a group playing games at a party, because I understand why I feel the way I do. It's not that I don't like to have fun or can't enjoy my friends. So I don't feel isolated. I just don't like to play games outside a counseling setting. Understanding why we do not at times feel as though we fit with certain people helps us to feel less threatened and therefore less lonely, for a confused feeling of isolation from others, seemingly without reason, breeds loneliness.

Certain general groups of people in this society have specific life-styles thrust upon them. By understanding that fact and structuring their lives accordingly, they can handle loneliness better. A single person can sometimes better handle evenings alone if he or she plans a social activity at the end of the week. Too often such people try to alleviate their loneliness by constant activity all week, which merely leaves them with a feeling of emptiness. Furthermore, the resultant fatigue makes them more vulnerable to any negative feelings, including loneliness.

But single people are not the only ones who must use structure in dealing with loneliness. Marriage can be a very lonely state, especially when the marriage is under stress. The loneliness of not being understood by the one you love can be greatly helped by having other friends and other activities apart from those directly related to the marriage. Too many married people give up friends and outside interests and devote all their energies to their family. Then they wonder why they feel so desperately dependent upon each other and so lonely when a problem within the marriage arises. Very often, people confide to me that when they have a problem they have no one to talk to except their spouse, and when the problem is the spouse there is no one to turn to. One woman whom I saw in counseling became involved in an afternoon Bible study once a week, where she made several close friends. Another woman now works part time. Another takes a class. But in addition to adding a diversionary activity to their lives, all these women were seeking out places where they could meet other women and be friends.

Married men have similar needs but have the advantage of meeting people at work. A job where one earns one's livelihood, however, is not always the best place to develop intimate friendships. Thus a startling number of men I meet know nothing of social intimacy apart from their wives. We Christians and others have always been caustically critical of men who go from work to bars and then home. Yet for some men it has been the best way they could find to have a quiet, alone time at the end of the day and to find some comradeship apart from demands and other people's needs.

In view of the extremely large percentage of extramarital relationships that I hear of in my office—*not* excluding Christians, Christian workers or the clergy itself—I am even more convinced of a person's combined needs of aloneness and companionship in order to survive loneliness. At the end of his day, the average American man comes home to children, a justifiably tired wife, and problems. No wonder he sneaks off to a bar or escapes into the arms of a relationship that seems, at least on the surface, to give something back to him. It is lonely to have your whole world demanding something from you as you come home from work. It is the loneliness of not being understood and of not being supported. It is also lonely to be the wife, performing the thankless, endless tasks of housework and engaging in five-year-old conversations. This, too, is the loneliness of not being understood by a husband who thinks he's the only one who worked all day. It is the loneliness of no adult companionship and, again, the loneliness of supporting a family emotionally and physically with no adult feedback and reinforcement.

A family structure that includes time for a wife and husband to be alone by themselves and together with each other and with friends will be a good antidote for loneliness as well as divorce and other family problems. The development of such a structure would have to be unique for each couple and family. A place as well as a time to be alone should be a top priority for every couple.

Husbands and wives should have occasional meals alone and weekends away. Additionally every man and woman needs to have time *alone* with a friend. Golf, lunch, shopping, sports events are all ways to develop relationships that depend upon outside friendships, not just those involved with the marriage. Then, of course, there should be the usual involvement with other couples and total family relationships.

But these are not our problem here. What we are focusing on now is the crying need we all have for privacy and intimacy apart from the group. Such privacy and intimacy help remove the feelings of loneliness that arise from isolation.

Apart from the varying needs of the two large categories of people, married and unmarried, smaller groups of people have special problems with loneliness that need structuring. There is a loneliness in fame, for example. The other day I watched a very famous talk-show host ward off autograph seekers while he was trying to have lunch and plan his next few shows. He was stared at, whispered about, paged on the telephone, and in general surrounded by people. But how lonely to have to perform even at lunch while you're trying to work out the format of your next few programs. For him, obscurity and remote spots would alleviate this loneliness caused by the crowds that pursued him. While dining out once a week might be good for a couple escaping the combined loneliness of job pressures and household demands, our talk-show host would only experience greater loneliness in a public place.

The specific loneliness of certain groups of people has been recognized in the formation of such common-interest organizations as Kiwanis, Weight Watchers, Alcoholics Anonymous, Teen Challenge, and so on. Again, commonality of needs and interests help alleviate loneliness. And a structuring that includes people with common life-styles is important in dealing with loneliness.

Whatever our uniqueness, we handle our loneliness best by planning our lives, not by overactivity. The life of Christ, as He functioned on this earth, offers a pattern for this. He was famous and dealt with the multitudes. He healed, preached to, and mingled with large groups of people. But he planned times of rest away from the mobs. He spent time alone with His Father and just away by Himself. He had an intimate relationship with three disciples and a very close one with the other nine disciples and with such friends as Mary and Martha. When someone like Judas failed, He had others to fill in the loneliness of loss. When all failed, as they did in the Garden of Gethsemane, He had His heavenly Father to draw upon. He planned times to be with these close friends; they didn't just happen.

Such structure is hard to achieve in our society. The average American today doesn't face his loneliness and try to resolve it. Instead he runs in an endless round of sometimes meaningless activity.

> He comes to feel that he is hopelessly trapped by circumstances beyond his control, that he is "stuck," that he has been defeated by life, that life is a rat race, a treadmill, and that there is a vast emptiness in him—Frankl's "existential vacuum." This vacuum exists among the rich and poor, the young and old, the successes and failures. As logotherapists could show, business executives try to fill it with extra work, their wives with parties and bridge games, students with marijuana or LSD. The existential vacuum lurks behind many of man's feverish attempts to fill his emptiness—with sex, alcohol, defiance of authority, speedy cars, committee work, television watching, overeating, and even with such respected activities as politics, psychoanalysis, and religion.[3]

I might add that, although we as a people feel profound loneliness, we also do not have the courage to confront that loneliness with a courageous no to inappropriate demands and a careful structuring of our lives that would better enable us to do our task, rather than detract from it.

Mike was a good friend of mine years back. He had been a junkie for years, but through coming to know Jesus Christ he had been able to get off heroin. Then he was able to help others who were as trapped in the drug world as he had been.

His schedule, if you want to call it that, was impossible. He was inundated literally day and night by desperate needs, and he always tried to meet them. He never said no. The Christian world respected him, and they should have, for he was a fine man. But the same people who lauded him for "burning out for God" usually made sure they had their lives better structured, with time for rest and recreation.

We talked one day, just as friends. He was tired and jagging himself up with coffee as usual. He was lonely and felt that he needed time and someone who understood him. I remember almost begging him to say no to some of the demands and to plan times with people who would nourish him. He shook his head almost hopelessly and said, "No, I can't turn anyone down. I know the hell of the drug addict too well." I felt hopeless too, for I knew that I couldn't reach him. For a moment in his loneliness he had reached out and been understood. Then, in a mistaken idea of God's plan for his life, he stepped back into the loneliness of trying to walk on water, into what Rollo May calls "the Messiah Complex."

I didn't see Mike again. A few weeks later a student recently off drugs came over to me and said: "Did you hear about Mike?"

"Hear about what?" I answered.

"He's dead. He died of an overdose," replied the student.

I thought it was a joke, a cruel joke, as I stood still in disbelief. Then numbly I took the newspaper clipping he handed me and I knew it was true.

"Jesus Christ can meet all your needs," I remembered Mike shouting at a group of high school students. Yes He can, I thought. But only if you let Him. But we have an awesome capacity to resist Him. Jesus Christ never meant for Mike to die in his twenties, but Mike wouldn't work out the details of his life in a way that would preserve it. It was a mistaken nobility, for in the long run he missed helping a lot of people in what could have been a long lifetime.

Ironically, there were indications that that night when Mike overdosed, he finally reached out in his loneliness to a friend who worked with drug addicts also and who had unplugged his phone. Mike had gone too far and waited too long, and within minutes the pills took effect and he was dead.

An effective life takes planning that takes into account all the varied needs of a human being. This requires self-discipline and realism. None of us walks on water. When we try to, we drown. And in our drowning we are lonely. God rarely means for us to burn out. He is a God of discipline, not of dissipation. He is the God who tells us to care for our bodies, because they are the temple of the Holy Spirit. He is the One who fed the multitudes instead of telling them to renounce their human needs and listen to Him while He preached. Fatigue and hunger breed loneliness, and God does not mean for us to live lives that are dragged out and tired.

Unfortunately, within Christian circles it has become popular and noble to be overextended and weary. An ulcer is a sign of success, and fatigue a badge of doing God's will. As we swallow our Gelusil and gulp our coffee, somehow we feel that this is what God wants.

The other day I was reading a book about a missionary doctor. In it there is a description of the physician's excellent progress in starting a medical center in one part of the county in which she worked. Then, without warning, the mission board decided to move her into the jungle to a broken-down medical complex. Her first response was normal: anger, refusal, feelings of denial. Then, because she thought that such emotions were unchristian and *because* she realized that moving into the jungle would be harder, she decided to follow the board's orders. The idea was, the more overextended, the more painful, the greater the spirituality involved. That philosophy is pushing the puritan ethic to the extreme, but it is deeply embedded in Christian thinking. This missionary doctor not only changed the whole thrust of her work on this basis, but she thanked the board for their confidence as she moved into a multiplicity of jobs entailing a 5:30 A.M. to 10:30 P.M. work schedule.

Last night I heard a well-known preacher utter the words:

"If you're having trouble in your life, maybe God wants you to push hard; if you're not making it, maybe God wants you to do more." In sharp contradiction to that statement, maybe God is asking us to put priorities on our lives and to do a quality job for Him. Perhaps our problem is that we produce quantity, rather than quality. Perhaps God is asking us to do the more difficult task of structuring our life. If so, the result will be a life consistent with the grace of God, a life lived in the calm of God's provision.

NOTES

1. *The Journal of John Wesley,* with Introduction by Hugh Price Hughes, M.A. (Chicago: Moody Press, 1974), p. 390.

2. Ibid., p. 405.

3. Joseph B. Fabry, *The Pursuit of Meaning* (San Francisco: Harper & Row, 1980), p. 120.

5

The Loneliness of Overextension

LAST NIGHT I had dinner with a friend whom I had not seen since college. Much has changed for both of us. We talked about the recent things in our lives: his teenage son, my books, our families. Then our conversation drifted to the past, the people we used to know, the places we had been. They are all different now. But what struck me with a sharp force was what he told me about the people we had both known who had become permanently disabled, who had been retired early because of illness, and those who had died young. Their misfortune was not what shocked me as much as the memory I retained of my earlier view of them. For, as a young person, I had admired each of them as a person who was energetic and achieving, with an endless ability to produce. I wanted to be like them, and I envied their ability to keep going when everyone else quit from sheer exhaustion.

At that time, I had followed fairly well in their footsteps. I, too, received my approval for my own high-wire living from people both within and without the Christian church. Taking more courses in college than was recommended, in addition to extra courses at a theological seminary, plus a lot of social life, a part-time job, and an almost full-time activity in the local church all seemed glamorous to me and to those around me, who admired it even more when they themselves couldn't keep up. For our society in general worships fast living, whether it be a high wire of productivity or of just so-called entertainment.

Living on a high wire is living beyond one's physical, emotional, and spiritual energies. It is overextending, trying to be all things to all men, to walk on water. The fallout from such living is varied: ulcers, emotional flip-outs, muscular tightness, exhaustion, depression, hopelessness, heart attacks, and even death. For each person the symptoms are different, but the cause is the same: the continuous overextension of oneself.

We may each live on a variety of high wires. A friend of mine runs from one social commitment to the next, exhausted, not even enjoying the activities. That is a high wire. A man I know works full time and takes on extra jobs that keep him up until four in the morning. That is another high wire. Still another man, who is in the pastorate, has a twenty-four-hour counseling service going in addition to his pastoral duties. That, too, is a high wire. A housewife keeps her children perfectly dressed at all times, has a spotless house, cooks gourmet meals regularly, and wonders why she can't be spontaneously energetic when her husband comes home from work. That is a high wire. Some high wires seem more glamorous and productive than others. But they all amount to overextension and eventual waste.

While not blaming speed itself for our problems, Viktor Frankl sees an emptiness within our being, a lack of focus, which causes our need to run. Joseph Fabry says in his book on Logotherapy:

> Speeding is what Frankl terms one of man's "centrifugal" leisure activities, an attempt to escape from himself, an aimless flying off in all activities. Frankl

advocates something that might be called "centripe-
tal" leisure activities, directed toward, not away from
man's center. Such activities allow man to confront
himself and the existential problems he faces. Each
man, Frankl says, ought to have his "private desert,"
some place where he can retreat to think about himself—it may be a room, a patch of grass under a tree,
a cottage in the woods, a beach. Speed, in the shape
of fast cars, can be used constructively to take him to
his "desert." Frankl drives his car, as fast as he can
and as often as he can, to his beloved Rax Mountains
where he spends hours walking and rock climbing, in
lonely contemplation or in company of his fellow
climbers.

Many people, he feels, evade such confrontations
with themselves; they plunge into meaningless activities to run away from their existential problems. This
is the way he sees it: During the day, their thoughts
are constantly interrupted by phone calls, secretaries,
social obligations, children, and the noises of leisure
—the hi-fi, the television, the news on the radio, the
sports newscast. Then, at night they are plagued
by what he calls "existential sleeplessness"; the
unfinished thoughts do not let them fall asleep. But
instead of taking advantage of this opportunity to
think through their problems, they take sleeping
pills. "They fall asleep but, at the same time, they
fall prey to the repression not of the instinctual but
of the existential issues of their lives." Many people
today, Frankl says, do not have the courage to be
lonely, to face and solve their existential questions;
they speed them away during the day and tran-
quilize them away at night.[1]

Frankl is correct when he refers to the need to "have the
courage to be lonely," to stop and face oneself. But there is

also a tremendous loneliness involved in high-wire living. For while there is a natural exhilaration in the pace, there is also an awareness of potential failure, of not making it, of wanting so badly to play God but knowing deep down that it is impossible.

One of my best examples of this comes from a three-year period, before I started my private practice, when I worked with teenagers who were on drugs. I was available night and day. I worked with groups of students adding up to one hundred and fifty in a school quarter, six hundred a year, eighteen hundred in the three years. Each new quarter only added to the groups, for former members came back and never really dropped off. I became acclimated to the drug scene: staying with someone on a bad LSD trip, pouring endless cups of coffee and orange juice, trying to figure out what someone was on when he or she called in the middle of the night, and attempting to help some of these teenagers get out of the abyss into which they had fallen without letting myself fall into the role of narc. It was a tense job.

A friendly physics teacher in the school where I worked used to come and coerce me into leaving for a snack or lunch, and once in a while, but rarely, I would unplug my home phone.

It was a high wire of dangerous dimensions. I loved it in a sense, but I felt physically awful most of the time, naïvely wondering how I could feel so permanently tired when, after all, I did enjoy my work! People praised me. How much good I was doing, they would say. It seemed rather immoral to quit, and so I kept on.

Then, one summer, I got a phone call from a young person who had just visited two of the teenagers who had been part of that eighteen hundred. They were now twenty, married, and the parents of one child, to whom they liked to feed drugs and watch his reactions. I stopped cold. There had been value in what I had done, I reasoned. At least these young people had known someone who belonged in the straight world and still cared. I had bridged our two worlds and had made them feel less lonely. Some had come out of the drug culture, and others later dared to turn back for help once they had been through prison a couple of times. A few had been caught after taking an overdose soon enough to save their lives. I had contributed to some of this good, but basically, working with eighteen hundred students, all I could and did do was bandage, and that was not enough. A high wire of living, yet not enough. It was at that time in my life that I began to make a commitment to the principle of quality, not quantity. For, while this principle had been a lifelong ideal of mine, I had, in reality, attempted to achieve both quality *and* quantity. My decision was to go into private practice, where I could help people change in a permanent way, rather than just offer emotional first aid. It was only the first step away from high-wire living, but it was at least that.

During the three years that I worked with these students, the loneliness was deep. I felt responsible for too many lives. I was supposed to have answers, both for the teenagers themselves and others who were involved with them. I took their failures as my own. I hurt when they hurt, and that was most of the time. For the most part, my support personally had to come from the few other people I knew who understood and cared about those in the drug culture.

What I do now is less lonely. For when I give, I can give a lot from a store of reserve. But I do not live my patients or my writing twenty-four hours a day. I take time to read, to be with people of different types, to listen to good music and to wander on the beach. In these ways and others I become restored. I have Frankl's "private desert," a place where I can refurbish my energies spiritually, physically, and mentally.

It seems apparent that Christians are particularly vulnerable to high-wire living. As stated earlier, Rollo May calls this tendency "the Messiah Complex." We feel obligated to produce the work of God instead of being reverently content to let Him do His own work through us. For not we but God is ultimately responsible for His work. And it is His work, not ours.

We Christians may not have what Frankl calls an existential vacuum, but we share in an existential loneliness when we do not focus our drive and energies within our Christian faith. We take the whole scope of God's plan and the whole scope of our own personal needs and interests and try to do them all. The result is failure, and we feel alone and rejected by God and man.

Yet, in spite of the overwhelming flood of counter opinion, some who have served God with conspicuous success have learned, even if the hard way, that they could serve God better if they did not burn out. Geraldine Taylor was the daughter-in-law of Hudson Taylor, the founder of the highly successful China Inland Mission (now known as the Overseas Missionary Fellowship). It fell to Geraldine to write a large number of the mission's books, among them a two-volume biography of Hudson Taylor. While her name has somewhat lost familiarity in recent years, her influence on the Christian church has been great. Her biographer, Joy Guinness, writes in a telling section about Geraldine's tendency toward high-wire living. It is instructive, perceptive, and balanced in its message. Says Joy Guinness:

> Any vital personality tends to become the pivot of a multitude of other lives. Geraldine's was no exception. . . . It is impossible to record these things; they are too many and too small, yet they fill the greater part of our days. . . .
>
> It is possible to live in the pressure of such things, and far more than these, perfectly serene, knowing that nothing happens by chance in a God-guided life, and that there is a sufficiency of grace for every claim. But a human life is limited, and there is always the danger of attempting too much.
>
> In 1904 Geraldine had undertaken more than she

was able to carry through. She had been writing the
Life of Pastor Hsi, and then had gone straight to a
long tour of speaking engagements. A letter from her
father shows to what it had led:

"We are so interested to hear of the wide acceptance your book on Pastor Hsi has met, and of its
being translated into six languages. It must be a rich
reward to you after your toils upon it. I think of your
writing so diligently in Switzerland when we were
with you, correcting and re-correcting page after
page. I do not wonder that you should feel now the
wearing effects of so much labour, and especially of
your missionary travel and meetings in America and
the United Kingdom. How well I understand that
nervous breaking down from which you have
suffered. Let it be a warning. There is a limit you
should not attempt to pass in exhausting labours. It
is not easy to fix it, but experience shows pretty
clearly where it is. I have gone beyond it at times,
when all the foundations of life seemed gone. I cannot express what that means, and hope you will
never know. Most people have no conception how
thin the foundations are which keep them above the
abyss, where the interests of life exist no more. I tell
you this, for you need to be warned. Learn to say
'No' to invitations or calls to labour which destroy
the power to labour and the possibility of service. I
do think Howard, as your husband—and doctor—
should say 'No' for you, and forbid suicidal toils ab-
solutely, firmly, finally. Tell him that with my sincere
love."

Howard was nothing loth to accept the charge,
and he fulfilled it faithfully for forty years—he hus-
banded her strength so well that at seventy-five she
was beginning work on her last biography.

A letter from Howard written in 1934 contains a

revealing passage: "Did I ever tell you of a time when my efforts to shield her from overwork were unwelcome? Seeing she was grieved, I asked her: 'Darling, where would you have been by now if I hadn't been taking care of you?' 'In my grave long ago,' she replied."[2]

After years of high-wire living, however, it is difficult to come down and live a paced, focused life. For one thing, such a process involves drastic change, which takes time and effort. It means a new way of living, and newness is always frightening, just because it is new. Instead of constantly rushing around, it means having space and time, which can also be frightening if it is a new experience.

Coming off a high wire can also involve disapproval and something none of us like to hear: the suspicion that we are becoming snobbish, aloof, lazy and, in general, just less dedicated than we used to be.

There may be feelings of guilt over not being able to be all things to all men, a guilt that is of course reinforced by any feelings of rejection coming our way. All these reactions may produce intense feelings of loneliness within the person getting off of the high wire, for he may not feel understood at all.

In addition to the feelings of loneliness that are produced by the newness, the disapproval, and the guilt, there is the equally deep isolation of working out the change itself. All these feelings are temporary as compared to the permanent loneliness of high-wire living, but nevertheless it is a lonely process to restructure one's life. This is especially true because most of us who overextend have a fairly deeply ingrained life-style built up, which is not easily altered.

In the alteration of a high-wire life-style, two factors are vital. One is the establishment of priorities, and the other is the declaring of those priorities. If one is a teacher, for example, it is necessary to teach during the day, attend some meetings, make out lesson preparations, and grade papers. If one adds social life, church and/or community duties and a part-time outside job, the load may be getting quite heavy. To say no, at this point, to serving on an additional committee may sound uncooperative, but in the end it is not so at all. It is survival, it is healthful selfishness, which preserves a person so that he can do his primary task well.

The mother who drives four children in four different directions each day, does her own baking, and belongs to every volunteer organization that seeks her help may be so overextended that she does nothing well and resents having nothing left for herself. She would be a better mother and member of the community if she set up priorities and established firmly what things constitute her real focus in life, saying no to those that do not fit in that category.

Saying no is somewhat easier if one is convinced of its appropriateness and if in saying no one realizes that the other person may or may not understand. The important thing is that no be said, not that the other person understand. Sometimes he or she does and that is nice; sometimes people even change; but their response is not the main focus.

Many people feel so trapped by high-wire living that they don't even try to change or perhaps don't believe that there is a possibility of such change occurring. In a recent issue of *TV Guide*, an article appeared on the high-wire living of a highly successful television producer. The article starts out with the following description of the results of such living:

> Only 10 days ago, he had left the hospital after quadruple-bypass surgery. No more would he be able to exist on a few hours' sleep a night and a diet of coffee, cigars and peanut-butter crackers. No more would he drive himself incessantly to craft what he thought was television's finest situation comedy. At 54 [he] was going to have to slow down.

Comments the producer himself:

"I knew I was burned out at the beginning of last season. . . . I knew, too, that people depended on me to do everything. So I'd created a very difficult situation. When you reach that point, what do you do?"[3]

This man stayed on the high wire and almost fell off permanently when he suffered a severe heart attack.

Catherine Marshall has indicated in one of her books that she believed that Peter Marshall was never meant to die so young.[4] As the pastor of the famous Church of the Presidents, in Washington, D.C., and as chaplain of the United States Senate, his influence was great. In the energy of his personality and drive, he was unstoppable. Finally, after a second heart attack, he died while yet a young man. There is no question of the sincerity of his walk with God or of the extent of his work. Yet he did burn out at a young age. One cannot help but wonder about the enormous scope of the work of Peter Marshall had he gotten off his high wire and paced his work through a longer lifetime.

For there is a principle of life that is true of all life and continues into the spiritual part of our existence: We have only so much force and energy; it can be used to do quality work that has depth, or it can be spread out so thin that nothing much is accomplished in spite of much exhaustion and effort. As Amy Carmichael put it, "Only God can plow both deep and wide."[5] Samuel Rutherford wrote a long time ago along the same lines: "There is but a certain quantity of spiritual force in any man. Spread it over a broad surface, the stream is shallow and languid; narrow the channel and it becomes a driving force."[6]

NOTES

1. Joseph B. Fabry, *The Pursuit of Meaning* (San Francisco: Harper & Row, 1980), pp. 119–20.

2. Joy Guinness, *Mrs. Howard Taylor, Her Web of Time* (London agents, Lutterworth Press: China Inland Mission, 1952 [reprint]), pp. 198–99.

3. Ron Nessen, "It's Live. It's Different. It's Drama—It's Real Life," *TV Guide*, Vol. 27, Issue #1371, p. 9.

4. Catherine Marshall, *A Man Called Peter* (New York: McGraw-Hill Book Company, Inc., 1951), p. 18.

5. Amy Carmichael, *Kohila* (Fort Washington, Pa.: Christian Literature Crusade, n.d.), p. 139.

6. Ibid., p. 139n.

6

The Loneliness
of Suffering

A CHRISTIAN YOUTH director sat across from me in a restaurant discussing his job and some projects we had in common. Finally our talk narrowed down to the problems that several young people in his high school youth group were having. Bluntly, almost abruptly, Ted stopped talking and then asked: "Can I talk to you about my own problem? Remember me, I'm the one people come to for advice. I have no one that would understand." And so we talked. Ted felt safe, and I felt profound empathy for this man upon whom so many leaned and yet who felt isolated in his own pain and hurts, with no one to turn to.

But pain is no respecter of age. Melissa was a four-year-old child who had already been placed in three different foster homes and had begun to learn that it was dangerous to count on permanence from anyone. On one particular day, Melissa was more quiet than usual. At the end of our hour, she resolutely sat down and said:

"I'm going home with you. I want to live with you and never leave."

I had been the only person who had not changed in my relationship with her and had not abandoned her. As she put it, "You've never left me. You're safe." It was very hard for her to understand why she couldn't live with me. It was hard for me to see her leave that office, unshed tears welling up in her tightly clenched eyes. Even though I had still not left her, in her mind I had in some way failed. She didn't understand, and in her pain she was once again alone, as she had so often been before.

Suffering appears to each of us uniquely and from its own, new source. Sometimes loneliness is derived from its very uniqueness. The youth director feels lonely in his suffering because he is a Christian leader, thus not part of the crowd. In contrast, during the earthquake in Southern California a few years ago, people suffered from deep fear but they were not generally lonely. Everyone had the same fear. There was a community of suffering in which each understood the others. It was socially acceptable to be afraid.

Death is an interesting study in loneliness. It represents universal suffering, for everyone is stung by the pain of the death of a loved one. Thus it is one of the most stereotyped examples of socially acceptable pain, and yet it, too, has its uniqueness, both in its manifestation and in its social acceptance. It is acceptable to suffer upon hearing the news of the death of a loved one. That pain culminates in the funeral service, which serves many purposes, ranging from a reverential remembrance of the loved one to a catharsis for the grief of those left. But try falling apart two weeks later—or six months. Then "It's time she got busy and started living again" or "My, she certainly hasn't handled Edward's death very well" are typical statements that will be made. Yet there are studies that indicate that the real impact of a bereavement often hits with greatest force about six months after the death, long after it is socially acceptable to grieve!

In countless other ways, we as a society have set up criteria for appropriate suffering. You can suffer with terminal cancer

but not with alcoholism or drug addiction. How many times
have you seen "John Doe requests prayer for his drinking
problem" posted in the church paper? No way. Any John Doe
is smarter than that. With all his problems, he doesn't need
the added problems of criticism and unlove. Yet, ironically,
while you don't generally connect Christians with overindulg-
ing so-called sinners or overempathizing with them in their
pain, such was the very quality for which Jesus Christ *was*
criticized. He ate with sinners and cared about the suffering
of sinners and was predictably criticized by the religious
world for his concern.

Great men of God down through history have met with
unjust criticism for their suffering. Charles Haddon Spurgeon,
whom most consider the greatest preacher in England during
the nineteenth century, endured painful depression during the
major portion of his life. Even Spurgeon himself spoke of his
suffering as a refining process that God often used to prepare
him for great service. Nevertheless, even those who were con-
verted to Christianity through his ministry at times failed to
understand how the great Spurgeon could also be depressed.
After all, aren't great men of God supposed to be happy all
the time? Of course, if they are, then even David, the writer
of the Book of Psalms, was a failure. For in spite of the fact
that he is the only person whom God called a man after his
own heart, he was profoundly depressed at times.

Job suffered for righteousness because God could trust him.
Yet his friends couldn't handle the unusual heaviness of the
suffering, so they told him to confess his sin. Somehow, when
you're suffering because you're good and even your best
friends think you have to be sinning, that is the acme of the
loneliness of suffering.

Thus, in our rigidity of right and wrong, appropriateness
and inappropriateness, we cause people who are suffering to
suffer even more because they are lonely in their isolation.
And we ourselves suffer too when our own pain does not fit
the mold, for sooner or later most of us suffer in this world.

In essence, each of us relates to pain we have ourselves experienced and therefore are familiar with. We are really saying, "You may hurt if you hurt like me." Oh, we don't say it so blatantly, but we say it. A father shouted at his little boy, "Stop that! You've cried all day!" It was as though since the child's pain had lasted beyond the time that fit the father's understanding, it couldn't be real. C. S. Lewis talks about the ease with which we can announce to a group of people that we have an aching tooth. But, continues Lewis, we would not be taken seriously if we claimed our heart was breaking. Furthermore, such a declaration would be considered inappropriate in a social group. Why should it be acceptable to discuss an aching tooth but not a breaking heart? Why Susie's braces but not John's drug problem? Why Margaret's open-heart surgery but not Philip's spiritual depression? Why should the physical be socially acceptable and understood and not the emotional? And why even with physical problems or such other acceptable problems as death do we have limitations imposed on how we should suffer and how long?

From our own experience and from what we learn very early in life of what society demands of us, we each learn how to suffer *within* society's limitations. And most of us just suffer more quietly when we go outside of those boundaries. When we begin to suspect that we have, like the little boy, "cried all day," we learn to hide our pain and hence the isolation of loneliness.

But it is often when pain is at its height, when we are suffering the most, that the thrust of not being understood hits the hardest. For if to share another's burdens is to do just that, to cut them in half, then to bear one's burdens alone is to intensify them.

A great part of the isolation of suffering arises when others not only do not understand us but, as if to reinforce their lack of understanding, impose solutions on us for which we are not ready or which really will not work. Dr. Paul Tournier offers a good illustration of this in his discussion of "places." Accord-

ing to Tournier, we each have our own place, that with which
we feel safe and are familiar. That place may be a belief, a
memory, a room, a house, even a country. And we change
places, but change may be painful, because it involves an un-
certain transition. When we have many places—friends, job,
recreational interests, family roots, and other areas where we
are at home and feel secure—a transition can mean growth
and becomes a good choice. But when the fabric of our life is
thin, we cannot change our place. To further amplify his
lengthy discussion of this point, Tournier gives the following
example:

> I have just had a letter from an old lady who has
> suffered a lot. Her husband was persecuted by the
> Nazis, and died in a concentration-camp. She has no
> children. Her only support was her flat, where she
> had all the things that reminded her of her happy
> years of long ago. In order to be nearer her friends
> she left her flat, and left the town without suspecting
> that this exile would plunge her into acute dis-
> tress. . . .[1]

At another point, Tournier illustrates his point when he
makes the therapy office a place for many. As he puts it, "Giving a place to those who have none!"
Continues Tournier:

> The giving of a place to those who have none
> seems to me to be one way of defining our vocation
> as healers of persons. As we have seen, one becomes
> a person only if he really has a place. So in helping
> our patients to find their places we are helping them
> to become persons. And that place is not abstraction.
> It is our consulting room, the fireside, the photo-
> graphs on the mantelpiece, the clock they detest, the
> books on the shelves, all the little details with which

they have become familiar during those hours that
have been so important in their lives. When I moved
house, one patient whom I had been treating for a
number of years took more than three months to feel
at ease in my new consulting room. And how many
patients find it hard to leave when the consultation is
over, to leave this place![2]

Yet those who are lonely are constantly advised to make
moves that take away their place. An elderly friend of mine
had lived, worked, and then retired, living in the same town
and apartment the entire time. The neighborhood became
run-down, and it was dangerous for her to take the long walk
to which she had become accustomed. Twice her purse was
snatched; once she was knocked down. Friends and family
insisted that she move near them, where it was "safe" and
where she could be "taken care of."

She moved and lapsed into a depression that two years later
is still present. Her loneliness is deep, but she is "safe." Safe
for what? one wonders. The advice of friends was based on
conventional logic: Old people need care and should be safe.
It did not understand her uniqueness. She had left a place of
pleasant memories, many of which were of people who are
now dead. She left her rose garden, her familiar old stove
upon which she used to cook family meals, the comfortable
porch with the rocking chair, and the sweet-pea vine outside
the back door. She left her place, her town, her stores, at the
advice of people offering stereotyped, seemingly appropriate
advice, and she is depressed and lonely. She feels no one understands, and she is not far from right.

It is possible, however, even in the midst of suffering, to alleviate some of the loneliness.

One of the most effective ways to handle suffering is to
change one's attitude toward it. In the twentieth century the
stories of the Nazi concentration camps are filled with inspiring reinforcement of the possibility of controlling one's atti-

tude toward suffering. Viktor Frankl became a product of the crucible of the camps. After losing almost all of his family, including his wife and parents, Frankl became refined into an instrument of hope to those immersed in the loneliness of suffering. Speaking of his own three years of internment in the camps, Frankl quoted the German poet Rilke: "Wie viel ist aufzuleiden!" (How much suffering there is to get through!)[3] Continues Frankl: "Rilke spoke of 'getting through suffering' as others would talk of getting through work."

And in getting through that suffering Frankl stressed the attitude one must take. "When a man finds that it is his destiny to suffer, he will have to accept his suffering as his task; his single and unique task. He will have to acknowledge the fact that even in suffering he is unique and alone in the Universe. No one can relieve him of his suffering or suffer in his place. His unique opportunity lies in the way in which he bears his burden."[4]

"The way in which he bears his burden," his attitude toward suffering—that is the key. And when a man can develop a reason for an attitude toward his suffering, he is no longer as lonely. The isolation diminishes because some of the pain of the suffering is alleviated. But, more than that, the isolation diminishes because now, in himself, the man understands his own suffering, and that understanding relieves him of some of his need for outward support. He can now endure. In the words of Nietzsche, "He who knows the *why* for his suffering can endure any *how*."

When my father died, five years ago, my mother felt deep loneliness and made such futile statements as, "Why did he have to die when he loved life so much?" Her loneliness increased as she saw other couples still enjoying each other while she was alone. Then gradually she began to move in another direction. She remembered how proud my father had been of his physical strength and knew he would not have handled the disabilities of age very well. She recalled his often-repeated fears of something happening to her and knew that he had been spared that suffering. In a sense, she had suffered for him, since one of them would have died sooner or later. As the reality of the purpose of her suffering became part of her thoughts and emotions, the pain and loneliness subsided. Her suffering had purpose. She had also found out that great secret of life, that everything ends, even pain, that this, too, shall pass. And as she passed out of that painful introspection that comes with intense suffering, she started to live in the practical, mundane world again, which further alleviated her loneliness.

For, as dull as one's daily task can sometimes become, one's task is a preserver of sanity. The absorption into one's task, the feelings of self-worth that arise from doing that task well all elevate our sense of self-worth and, again, help the feelings of loneliness to at least diminish. For my mother, the task she returned to was oil painting. Then she did some exhibits and started teaching art to a student. These contacts flowed into some new social relationships. Not only the suffering but necessarily the loneliness of that suffering began to heal.

For Frankl, the task was wound up in his being a psychiatrist and in his views on suffering itself. For as the development of an attitude toward suffering had helped him survive, he now turned that belief into a new philosophy for psychotherapy—Logotherapy—and the propagation of that school of thought became part of his life task.

Our suffering often cannot be avoided. It hits so often when we least expect it. It seems strange and new. We feel that perhaps no one else has ever suffered in quite the same way. We feel unique and alone. And there is a sense in which that is true, for no one else has ever been or will ever be quite like us. But that uniqueness has the potential for unique growth, for finding unique meaning, for performing a unique task. I have at times severe allergic reactions to chemicals, drugs, or foods. It has the feeling of a unique form of suffering when you start choking for air and hope medication works in time. It feels unique to travel in a strange country, hoping no new insect spray or food additive will cause some biochemical chaos. But the loneliness of those feelings have helped me realize how alone each of us feels when she or he hurts.

Particularly in my work with drug addicts, this personal background has had meaning for me in the performance of my task. I understand the fear of a bad LSD trip, although I have never taken LSD. For once you have felt that out-of-control feeling in your body, you can relate to those of the drug culture.

If one's attitude toward suffering and the use of one's task help remove the loneliness in suffering, linked to these is the development of relationships with other people.

Some people won't understand. That is true, and that fact accentuates the loneliness. But, although no one else can ever get into our skin, even if he wants to, there are people who understand, and we must find them.

A woman left my office the other day expressing relief when I told her that many of the hidden, painful feelings she was experiencing were normal and had been felt by various other people. Her suffering and loneliness in that suffering were alleviated by understanding from another human being who was basically saying that she was okay and not alone.

A good therapy session often alleviates the loneliness of suffering, for while the pain may still exist, the comradeship of another person who gives support in the middle of pain greatly helps in handling suffering.

A good friendship has some of the same effect, except that a friend does not exist for our growth and in some ways his responsibility toward us does not extend as far as that of a therapist. But the idea of support among friends is vital to life in all its phases, especially in suffering. According, once again, to Dr. Tournier:

"That the weak, the lonely, the neurotic, people who have always lacked support, should seek it avidly, is obvious and easy to understand. But the strong need it quite as much. It is less noticeable, because they hide it more easily. . . ." But, explains Tournier, "We cannot live without support. . . ."[5]

And when life offers its most difficult times, what do we hold onto then? "In these circumstances what can I make my support as I start off once more? What can I use as a thread to guide me forward through the darkness of this moment? I need a sort of radar that would enable me to take off and land blind. That radar, I think, is my conviction that God has a purpose for me, a purpose for each one of us, and at every moment of our lives. I believe that God can lead me, even when I cannot yet see the road clearly in front of me. . . ."[6]

The support of God and man can make any suffering seem less lonely. Yet we in the Christian church would do well to examine our own view of suffering before we inflict that view on those in pain. Do we indeed think that suffering implies sin, as did Job's friends and some modern-day Christians, who tell me that most of my patients wouldn't need counseling if they were right with God? Or can we agree with Charles Spurgeon that, in his words, "God cannot make ministers . . . except in the fire"? Continues Spurgeon: "It is then, and there alone, that He can make His sons of consolation; He may make His sons of thunder anywhere, but His sons of consolation He must make in the fire, and there alone. Who shall speak to those whose hearts are broken, who shall bind up their wounds, but those whose hearts have been broken also . . . ?"[7]

Do we simplistically assume that people who don't respond to our help instantly "just don't want to feel better" or "enjoy having something to complain about"? As though some people just enjoy suffering! No one enjoys suffering. I knew a young girl who carved her arms whenever she was upset. Another young person burned herself with cigarettes. Neither of them liked pain. They just hurt so badly with all the stored guilt and self-hate that to be cut or burned was to transfer the greater pain to a lesser one. They were getting rid of pain, although certainly in a very inadequate fashion! I'm not so sure that we who function in areas of mental-health treatment were not partially responsible for this attitude that some people like to suffer when we invented such nondescript terms as masochism. In the truest sense of its meaning, no one likes pain. Perhaps if our friend seems to be nursing his or her wounds it is because there are so many deeper wounds that have not been attended to and would be even more painful if they were faced.

Suffering is an integral part of all existence, as is loneliness. And so many times they are interrelated until the one seems to become the other. But suffering that is supported by the radar of God's purpose and the understanding of sensitive friends can at least be free of that deep, nonrelenting feeling of loneliness. And then, at the end of any deep suffering, there is, I think, a little of the feeling of the person freed from those concentration camps when "The crowning experience of all, for the homecoming man, is the wonderful feeling that, after all he has suffered, there's nothing he need fear anymore—except his God."[8]

NOTES

1. Paul Tournier, *A Place for You* (New York: Harper & Row, Publishers, 1968), p. 165.

2. Ibid., p. 79.

3. Viktor E. Frankl, *Man's Search for Meaning* (New York: Simon & Schuster, Inc., Publishers, 1959), p. 78.

4. Ibid.

5. *A Place for You, supra,* p. 170.

6. Ibid., p. 167.

7. Charles H. Spurgeon, *The New Park Street Pulpit* (London: The Banner of Truth Trust, 1964), Vol. 4, pp. 460–61.

8. *Man's Search for Meaning, supra,* p. 93.

7

A Place to Be

SEVEN-YEAR-OLD Cathy had not seen me for two weeks, not since her mother had died suddenly in a freak car accident in which no one else had even been hurt. Once the funeral was over, she had not been allowed to cry, because her crying upset her father. In their grief her family had generally neglected to regard the pain of a small child. She had no place of safety in which to express her grief.

As soon as Cathy stepped into my office that day, she began to cry. The tears continued throughout the hour. There were few words. There was indeed little need for words. To be held and to express her feelings were what Cathy had needed for days. And this was her place emotionally and geographically to meet this need.

Part of alleviating loneliness lies in having places. These places can vary in type. A place can be an attitude that feels safe and right. It can be a relationship that is healthy and nourishing. Actual places, such as one's birthplace or a childhood haunt or just a familiar location, can provide this place to be.

Usually, if we are conscious of the process, we will find that security for most of us lies in the places that we find in all these different areas. For example, there is a deep insulation from loneliness in the steadfastness of our attitudes. All through my earlier life I had held on tenaciously to the notion that all church people, mainly church leaders, were to be respected. Then I began to meet some whom I could not respect. This was no mere matter of disagreement. What occurred were obvious breaches of any basis for trust. A basic attitude of mine had been shattered. And with that shattering came a sense of disillusionment and of loneliness. Something I had always believed in was gone. The unfamiliar had passed and in its place would come a new idea, a scary one because it was new. I would have to move to a new place.

People, too, provide places. And we move from these places too, for little in this life is permanent. Death robs us. Betrayal causes us to move on. Change motivates us to relinquish or to alter a relationship. A six-year-old girl had watched her father beat her mother. Later she said to me, "I wish he'd die. But maybe I could see him first." She was angry and wanted to be rid of this man whom she had learned to fear. Yet a part of her didn't want to lose this relationship, this place, which had been so important to her for six years. For a new person or place was unknown and scary. Change is lonely.

Last weekend, I went to a little town south of where I live. I stayed by the ocean for two nights in a cottage I discovered about three years ago. It has often provided a place of respite and work for me. But, in the past ten months, I had not had time to go there. It had been my place—but after ten months I wasn't sure that I would still feel that way.

My fears were partially well founded. The town had changed. There was a new proprietor at the motel. My favorite restaurant was under new management. My special gift shop had sold out. But I learned something new about places. We don't always just keep or lose our places. Sometimes they just become altered, and we only completely lose our place if

we reject the alterations. I discovered that the new proprietor
of the motel had a remarkable talent in art, and I enjoyed
looking through his paintings. My cottage was still right on
the ocean, as it had always been. The favorite restaurant was
actually much nicer under new management. Only the special
gift store seemed really worse for the change. I would miss
parts of the old, but much of the new had simply made my
place even better. I had not lost it. It had changed; a little
had been lost, but much had been gained.

Sometimes, however, whether they be beliefs, attitudes,
people, or actual geographical places, we lose our places. We
lose the anchors that hold us to the familiar. To use Alvin
Toffler's words, we lose our security zones.

There are many reasons for losing our place. And most of us
have many places, some more significant than others. More
often than not, the loss of one or two places does not devas-
tate us unless they are highly significant. And the normal
course of life seems to include the occasional loss of a place. It
is when a place that we cherish more deeply than others is
lost or when numbers of places are lost at one time, that the
problems may arise. The transition from lost to new becomes
frightening and seemingly impossible.

Such feelings are often experienced in a divorce, particularly if the loss is unexpected and fast. A woman who seeks
professional help after a series of beatings may long ago have
given up a relationship that she had felt was meaningful at
one time. The pain of divorce is less because she has left that
place slowly and it lost its meaning early in the process. On
the other hand, the man who comes home to find his wife in
bed with his best friend may suffer for a long time from his
sudden loss of a place. The leaving of such a place would be
felt acutely, because it had such significance in his life and
was lost abruptly.

At times the change of a place is forced upon us. A city
changes and the traveler returning to see his familiar birthplace is disillusioned when he finds something entirely differ-

ent. A job is terminated because of changing economic needs within the industry. A friend moves away or dies. People change and their change forces us to view them differently.

But equally we sometimes choose to lose a place because that place loses its value or actually becomes harmful. It no longer alleviates loneliness but, rather, it creates loneliness. One of my favorite aunts was a secure place to me as I was growing up. She told me stories about her work as a missionary in China and listened to my ideas and thoughts, childish as they must have been at times. As I grew up she was still a special person to me. She couldn't solve my adult problems the way she had helped with so many of my childhood ones, yet she still provided a place of comfort for me. She approved of me. She listened to me. And she loved me as someone very special.

Then, as she got quite elderly, she developed severe hardening of the arteries. She became forgetful and unable to care for herself. It was a slow process and so, protective of my place, I denied what was happening for as long as I could. Then my first book was published and I raced over to tell her. She smiled and asked an irrelevant question. Near tears, I finally realized. I had lost my place. Something I had shared with her and we had both wanted had happened, the publication of a book. Yet now she couldn't even comprehend that fact. She loved me still. But she no longer understood and she never would again on this earth. I had lost an important place. She still lived and I had responsibilities to her. But seeing her now reminded me of the old relationship, and it increased my loneliness rather than helped it. The answer was not to hope that things would improve. They wouldn't. Real hope lay in giving up that place and growing beyond it to a new place.

It is at this point of losing places that psychotherapy can become a place not only in itself but as a bridge between the old that has been left and the new that will replace it. It is a growing point, a safety spot between the known and the new.

American society is in general a lonely society. We isolate ourselves and stress our rights and then wonder why we feel independent and remote from others. We help people through impersonal welfare agencies and fear the involvement of personally helping a stranger in need. We have experienced a deep breakdown of the family unit and then develop various forms of communal living so as not to be alone. I encounter many widows who live within blocks of each other, each bemoaning their individual loneliness. Several of them have complained about their large, empty houses. Yet each has turned down any idea I have offered to them of taking in students who need temporary homes. They prefer their loneliness to the risk of involvement.

In such a social climate, psychotherapy has flourished. Added to the social change has been also the impoverishment of the organized church. The resultant lack of meaning for many people has driven them in their existential loneliness to seek the help of the psychological community, rather than that of the religious order, which they may feel has already failed them. Hence the growing popularity of psychotherapy. As such, psychotherapy has become an important place for many, a place where if the therapy is healthy and valid, the loneliness of change is alleviated. It is a temporary place, until more permanent places are developed.

To start with, even the geographical place where therapy takes place becomes important. I have noticed that people tend to sit in the same chair in my office and become somewhat disoriented by a change of office. The time, the place, the setting, with all of its components of lighting, furniture arrangement, and general environment becomes a security factor in a person's world, where the change and loss may have already become overwhelming.

But it is, of course, the relationship with the counselor that becomes the primary place of importance. Rollo May expresses this relationship better than anyone else I know:

It raises the prestige of the one who is understood, and helps give him a sense of worth as a person. This understanding breaks down the barriers which separate man from his fellows, it draws the other human being for a moment out of the loneliness of his individual existence and welcomes him into a community with another soul. It is like inviting the traveler in from his snowy and chilly journey to warm himself for an hour before the fire on another's hearth. Such understanding, it is not too much to say, is the most objective form of love. That is why there is always a tendency on the part of the counselee to feel some love toward the counselor, this person "who understands me." There are few gifts that one person can give to another in this world as rich as understanding.[1]

Yet Dr. May does not overestimate the importance of the place of psychotherapy. For while it should be a place of safety and recovery and thus curative of loneliness, it is not guaranteed to always be that. It, too, can fail, like everything else in this world. And to feel loneliness in the place of therapy is indeed to feel a devastating loneliness. Dr. May's rather humble estimate of the potential of therapy in itself sheds hope.

Says Dr. May:

Finally, after all our discussion, we come to the realization that there is a great area in the transformation of personality which we do not understand, and which we can attribute only to the mysterious creativity of life. . . . As the matter has it, "The physician furnishes the conditions—God works the cure." Like the doctor, we may bind up the wound; but there are all the forces of life welling up in their incalculable spontaneity in the growing

together of skin and nerve tissues and the reflowing
of blood to perform the healing. Before the creative
forces of life, the true counselor stands humbly. And
his humility is not of the false sort, for the deeper his
understanding of personality the more clearly he realizes how minute his efforts in comparison to the
greatness of the whole. He says with the psalmist,
"Lord, that is too wonderful for me." I am myself
frank to say that when the limits of my own understanding are reached, I understand the miracle of
transformation of personality in terms of the age-old
but ever new concept, the grace of God.[2]

One of the factors that makes therapy a place, a bridge over
a loss of place, is that it is a predictable place of freedom and
safety. I notice this most graphically in children, for children
sometimes express feelings that adults have but are ashamed
to verbalize. To a child, this is his hour. He is safe uttering
ideas for which he would be punished in the outside world.
Some children become clock watchers, making such comments
as "That clock is broken, isn't it? I just got here." They demand rights, like the child who had to go to the bathroom but
ordered me to stay right where I was because his hour wasn't
over yet. Sometimes the comments are more poignant, such as
"Maybe I could just stay here forever" or, in an effort to
reserve me for herself, one child's plea of "Please don't let
anyone play here until I come back."

We all have a child in us, who in our pain craves a place
where it is, so to speak, our hour, our person, our place to be.
In a good therapy relationship, there should be that total freedom to be who we really are without feeling a loss of dignity
or a sense of disapproval. That does not mean that in therapy
we are not often confronted with the reality of our flaws and
challenged to change, for good therapy must at times involve
confrontation. But confrontation with dignity and respect
does not result in feelings of denigration but, rather, in a

greater sense of self-acceptance. And it is in the realization that this person, this therapist, really knows you and yet respects you that loneliness is dissipated and the place of therapy becomes a step to other places of stability in your life. For therapy is a very special place, a place of transition to other places.

Five-year-old Paul had been in therapy for two years after multiple drastic changes in his life. Now, after a period of calm it looked as though his parents might divorce. To him that was one change too many. When he came to my office that week he immediately started talking.

"My friend upset me this week," he started. "He called you my friend."

A little confused, I questioned him further as to why that had upset him.

With the seriousness of an eighty-year-old man, Paul continued, "Because you're my *therapist*, not my friend. Oh, you're a friend. But you're mostly my therapist."

I understood. Paul had lost many friends in his five years of life. He had also lost two fathers, several houses, relatives, and foster homes. He had lost many places. Therapy was a place that had been there throughout all the losses. It had always cushioned the pain. He had cried, laughed, yelled, remained silent, all in safety. Now his friend had told him I was a friend, not a therapist. And in his young mind a friend could not be trusted, a therapist could. No, he was not ready to change his place. For until there were more places, his relationship with me was his chief security zone, his safest place to be. In it he could ward off some of the loneliness of being only five in a world that was changing far too fast.

Indeed, for most of us the world is changing far too fast, particularly in this century, in this country. We cannot hold back the tide of circumstances and time, but we can develop our places to ward off the resultant loneliness. At times some of us may choose the place of psychotherapy because, like Paul, we find in it a temporary bridge to new places to be.

We will not eradicate our loneliness in so doing, but we will find insulation from much of its pain and from that spot will reach out to other places that will enable us to live beyond the extreme loneliness of this age.

NOTES

1. Rollo May, *The Art of Counseling* (Nashville: Abingdon Press, 1967), p. 119.

2. Ibid., p. 162.

8

Beyond the Place
of Psychotherapy

ANNETTE WAS AN attractive twenty-eight-year-old computer technician who had lost many places in her reasonably short lifetime. Finally, in the desperation of loneliness, she came in for several counseling sessions. During those times, she started to relax and to find the beginning of a new focus in her life. Then, one day, with as much determination as she had shown when she started counseling, she quit. Her reason? "I've never in my life trusted anyone. I'm beginning to trust you and that scares me. Maybe someday I'll come back. But until then I don't want to take the chance of depending on anyone."

Annette had the feeling that seeking professional counseling involves a loss of one's self, a giving up of one's place within one's self. In actuality the reverse should be true. One's place within one's self should grow stronger in counseling and there should be the additional discovery of new places beyond the doors of that office. There are, however, many misconceptions about this place, psychotherapy, both within and without the Christian community. These go beyond what is true of a good psychotherapeutic relationship and become reasons for hindering its potential to help.

One misconception is that people with deep pathology go to a therapist and everyone else is "normal," whatever "normal" is! Such an attitude is unnecessarily isolating. Actually, I know a great number of people who have a real need for psychotherapy but who could never begin to admit that need. Conversely, many people who consult me have no "deep pathology" but simply want to grow in some way or are suffering some pain from a variety of sources. Many are simply seeking a place to be while they establish new places in their lives. In the long run, they suffer less pain, because they generally solve their problems more quickly and more effectively than they would without therapy. Frequently even the cost is not as great as would be their loss of income from decreased productivity in their jobs or from increased medical bills, which often result from stress.

It is true that people with severe emotional problems seek psychological help. But to generalize that into the notion that most people in therapy are terribly sick is like saying that most people who enter hospitals with physical ailments are terminal. People seek medical help for colds and earaches as well as cancer and bubonic plague!

Another myth about psychotherapy is the crutch theory. It goes something like this. Therapy is a crutch, an emotional dependence, a form of weakness. Ironically, these same people would consider a person unbalanced if he walked around on a broken leg *without* a crutch. We all need to use crutches from time to time. They are good, for they allow the injured part to rest and recover. Permanent crutches are another thing. They cripple. But that is not what we are considering here. Having a maid for a week after a woman returns home with a new baby is a crutch. An understanding friend during a crisis, a meal brought in during a bout of the flu, an aspirin for a headache, ice cubes for a sunburn, a devotional reading on a down day—all of these are crutches. But they are hardly weakening or destructive. Psychotherapy is little more than these. It is a help through a rough spot, a source of growth into even greater independence, a place to recover and go on.

Christians have their own special hang-ups about psycho-therapy. These revolve mainly around the mistaken concept that psychology and Biblical theology are antithetical to each other. While it is obvious that certain teachings of some schools of psychology and certain teachings of some branches of the organized church are in conflict, Biblical theology and basic psychological truth are quite consistent with each other. Nor is it only the psychologists who have gone off on tangents. For within the church there exist some pretty irrational psychological attitudes.

Functioning in a black-and-white mentality, certain preachers and even so-called "Christian counselors" are very free in labeling emotional problems as sin in a fashion reminiscent of years back when certain of the clergy taught that physical illness was sinful. We are told to confess our depression and are led down a disillusioning path that promises that, for the Christian, life is indeed a rose garden. God, you may be 'sure, has never promised that. But well-meaning Christians do, and then wonder why people turn away from God months after a conversion that has led to disappointment in a Christian life that hasn't turned out to be the panacea that was promised.

Yet this current trend of superficial Christianity, which offers God as a giant aspirin and disparages Christians who seek professional counseling, is not typical of basic Christian thinking. Charles Spurgeon has always had the acclaim of the entire Christian community. Yet he suffered from black depressive spells. Spurgeon himself discredited in his preaching the idea that depression was sin. Aptly he pointed out such Biblical figures as David and such historical church figures as Martin Luther, who also suffered from depression and were not sinning. Spurgeon came to look at depression as something caused by overwork or lack of recreation or as a result of spiritual warfare. He saw it as part of God's refining process but not as sin. One gets the perhaps presumptuous feeling that Spurgeon might have had fewer problems with certain modern psychologists than with certain present-day Christian spokesmen.

What we Christians really have a hard time dealing with, both in ourselves and in others, is our humanity. We think in terms of sin and perfection, and we are afraid to admit that we have frailties, imperfections that have nothing to do with sin. We fear and tremble, and all but give up, and then add to our pain by feeling that God is angry with us. Actually, God is a God of precise balance. His is an awesome righteousness that abhors sin, and one might well fear to flaunt one's own sinfulness before such a One. But we must be honest about the nature of sin. Sin is untruth, murder, adultery, and all those things we hear preached about so much. But sin is also unlove, readiness to judge others, rudeness, and indifference to the needs of others.

The other aspect of God is His tenderness and love, a love that understands and does not further humiliate us in our imperfection. It is in this imperfection that psychotherapy can so often be of major assistance. Furthermore, we should not spend so much time debating whether God or psychology has an answer to the problem of sin. Instead, we should admit that not everything we call sin is sin. And perhaps some forms of behavior that have escaped the label of sin should be so designated even at the price of our discomfort!

C. S. Lewis had a magnificent balance on the types of imperfection. For example, when a lady with whom he was corresponding faced surgery and was fearful, instead of telling her to confess her fear he wrote, "Fear is horrid but there's no reason to be ashamed of it. Our Lord was afraid (dreadfully so) in Gethsemane. I always cling to that as a very comforting fact."[1]

It seems important to insert here one of Lewis' most clearly stated viewpoints on this whole debate between sin and imperfection, a viewpoint that clearly shows the difference between the two.

When a man makes a moral choice two things are involved. One is the art of choosing. The other is the various feelings, impulses and so on which his psychological outfit presents him with, and which are the raw material of his choice. Now this raw material may be of two kinds. Either it may be what we call normal: it may consist of the sort of feelings that are common to all men. Or else it may consist of quite unnatural feelings due to things that have gone wrong in his subconscious. Thus fear of things that are really dangerous would be an example of the first kind: an irrational fear of cats or spiders would be an example of the second kind. The desire of a man for a woman would be of the first kind: the perverted desire of a man for a man would be of the second. Now what psychoanalysis undertakes to do is to remove the abnormal feelings, that is to give the man better raw material for his acts of choice: morality is concerned with the acts of choice themselves.

Put it this way. Imagine three men who go to war. One has the ordinary natural fear of danger that any man has and he subdues it by moral effort and becomes a brave man. Let us suppose that the other two have, as a result of things in their subconsciousness, exaggerated, irrational fears, which no amount of moral effort can do anything about. Now suppose that a psychoanalyst comes along and cures these two: that is, he puts them both back in the position of the first man. Well it is just then that the psychoanalytical problem is over and the moral problem begins. Because, now that they are cured, these two men might take quite different lines. The first might say, "Thank goodness I've got rid of all those doo-dohs. Now at last I can do what I always wanted to do—my duty to my country." But the other might say, "Well, I'm very glad that I now feel mod-

erately cool under fire, but, of course, that doesn't
alter the fact that I'm still jolly well determined to
look after Number One and let the other chap do the
dangerous job whenever I can. Indeed one of the
good things about feeling less frightened is that I can
now look after myself much more efficiently and can
be much cleverer at hiding the fact from the others."
Now this difference is a purely moral one and psychoanalysis cannot do anything about it. However
much you improve the man's raw material, you have
still got something else: the real, free choice of the
man on the material presented to him, either to put
his own advantage first or to put it last. And this free
choice is the only thing that morality is concerned
with.

The bad psychological material is not a sin but a
disease. It does not need to be repented of, but to be
cured. And by the way, that is very important.
Human beings judge one another by their external
actions. God judges them by their moral choices.
When a neurotic who has a pathological horror of
cats forces himself to pick up a cat for some good
reason, it is quite possible that in God's eyes he has
shown more courage than a healthy man may have
shown in winning the V.C. When a man who has
been perverted from his youth and taught that cruelty is the right thing does some tiny little kindness,
or refrains from some cruelty he might have committed, and thereby, perhaps, risks being sneered at by
his companions, he may, in God's eyes, be doing
more than you and I would do if we gave up life itself for a friend.

It is well to put this the other way around. Some of
us who seem quite nice people may, in fact, have
made so little use of a good heredity and a good upbringing that we are really worse than those whom

we regard as fiends. Can we be quite certain how we should have behaved if we had been saddled with the psychological outfit and then the bad upbringing, and then with the power, say, of Himmler? That is why Christians are told not to judge. We see only the results which a man's choices make out of his raw material. But God does not judge him on the raw material at all, but on what he has done with it.[2]

Black and white? Hardly! Intolerant? Never! Yet Lewis states magnificently the grays within the human personality and within Christian thinking. It is good for all of us that we stand before God alone, Who has higher standards of righteousness than any of us and yet Who judges us by our motives, our capacities, our level of temptation. For God understands the imperfection of humanity. It is in the integration of such a theology of balance as well as compassion with a rational concept of psychology that people can be helped. For when one holds this viewpoint, there is no basic conflict between psychology and Christian theology.

A while back, I received a long-distance phone call from a young man whom I had never met. He had found an article of mine on Christians and psychotherapy in a laundromat and wanted to know if I could refer him to someone where he lived. "I've wanted psychological help for several years," he said, "and so has my girl friend but we were told that it was wrong for us as Christians. I'm so glad I read your article," he continued, "and that I can get help without feeling I've failed as a Christian."

I was glad for him, and hoped he would find someone who could help him, for I have a healthy skepticism about some of the poor and even destructive potential of some psychotherapy, and unfortunately I really didn't know anyone practicing in his town. Yet I felt sad, too, that someone like him who really wanted to grow and change had been forced to wait because of the personal bias of certain Christians with whom he had been in contact. In contrast, it would seem to me that Christians, above all other people, ought to have an optimism and enthusiasm about their personal growth, spiritually and emotionally, and that should include a willingness to use any method God makes available. For psychotherapy can become an important place—a place to be understood, to be heard, to be helped. It is a place in the midst of many places. And Christians, too, need this place to be.

For there is a healthy place beyond the place of psychotherapy, and that is to be found in the use of psychotherapy as a model for other life relationships.

A while ago, I saw a cartoon in a magazine that showed a sign posted over a psychiatrist's office saying, LOVE FOR SALE. The implications are obvious, but the meaning is not real, not for the kind of therapeutic relationship we have been considering. For a relationship between a therapist and his patient must be genuine if it is to have optimal results. And many of us who help people on a full-time basis would indeed prefer not to have to charge if there were an automatic way to live without charging.

The relationship is genuine, and accepting it does become an excellent model for life in general. In it many people learn to trust and be open for perhaps the first time in their lives. At times, they discover their uniqueness as well as their lack of uniqueness. They learn that some of their deepest, most inadmissible thoughts are not so unusual or strange after all. In general they learn that they are okay.

The same result should come out of a good friendship. It is true that the depth of exposure will not usually be the same. Nor is there a one-sided commitment from one person to help the other. Rather, there is a balance of give and take. But the ideas of trust, privacy, respect, and encouragement become a model from psychotherapy that should extend into other human relationships, which in turn become other places to be.

It is true that there are misconceptions that exist about psychotherapy and mental health in general. These prevent some people from ever finding therapy as a bridge from one place to another. There is the stark reality of the possibility of poor therapy, ineffective therapy and even destructive therapy. Again, a place, a bridge, a needed place of transition is denied to those who fail to perceive that such therapy is beyond the place that psychotherapy was meant to occupy. It is not a bridge or a place of restoration. For, in its failure, such therapy only deepens the loneliness of not being understood or of being beyond help. At times, it can cripple and become a permanent place, because progress is never made to the other places of life, and in so doing it goes beyond the proper place of psychotherapy.

But there is also therapy that helps people cope with a world that in truth is lonely. For them, therapy provides a place of refuge and growth. And for them, therapy can be the beginning of healthier relationships outside of the therapy session. For therapy is only meant to be a place of transition. To make it more than this is to go beyond the intended place of psychotherapy. On the other hand, to use it as a springboard into other, more meaningful places is to go beyond the place of psychotherapy in a most positive way.

A little boy had come to me after multiple illnesses and subsequent failure in school. He could not participate in sports and was generally ignored by most of the children. His sessions with me became his place to vent his anger and talk about the frustration of his failure. Months later he was ready to quit counseling. His physical health had improved, his grades were up, and he had friends. More and more, he found himself having to miss baseball games and fun with friends in order to have time to see me. After some resistance he finally agreed with me and his parents. It was time to quit. The next Wednesday afternoon, he played baseball with his friends. He had found a new place beyond the place of psychotherapy. When I saw him briefly a year later, I was glad. He now had his places with other people and other interests. His relationship with me had been an important place of transition, but that is all it was meant to be. That is all it is ever meant to be.

NOTES

1. C. S. Lewis, *Letters to an American Lady* (Grand Rapids: Wm. B. Eerdmans Publishing Company, 1967), p. 129.

2. C. S. Lewis, *Mere Christianity* (London: Geoffrey Bles, Ltd., 1962), pp. 71–73.

9

Loneliness in Intimacy

I WAS AT THE home of an English professor who lived on a hill overlooking the ocean not far from the university I attended. At that time, I was involved in such things as symbolism in Melville and the journals and diaries of early American writers. A group of us had been invited to the home of this particular professor in order to hear a lecture on some of the more obscure works of T. S. Eliot. I was bored but trying hard not to look bored. Since the lecture was obviously going to last for a couple of hours, I felt justified in taking a moment's break outside in the fresh air away from the smell of pipe tobacco. As I stepped out the front door, I abruptly encountered my English professor apparently taking the same welcome break. Our eyes met for a second, then a sheepish grin appeared on both our faces. In that instant we said nothing, but we said it all: I'm bored. I don't even understand this lecturer who's so impressed with his intellectuality that his words are pedantic and, at times, meaningless. I accept you if you're bored too. We never did verbalize how we felt, but we did earnestly debate who should "miss" the lecture a little longer in order to make coffee for everyone!

Many years later, I was standing at my father's bedside several weeks after he had two massive strokes. He could not talk, but he could show emotion through his hands and facial expressions. Not knowing how much of what I said he understood, I reminded him of a specialist whom he used to know and like and asked him if he'd like that man brought in.

Vehemently he showed disapproval in his face, and a deep understanding swept over me. He of course still liked and respected the named specialist. But he knew more than I did how close to death he was. He had fought hard, but now he had relinquished his hold on life, not hopelessly but realistically, and he wanted me to do the same. For the last time on this earth, our thoughts and feelings met and merged into oneness for a few brief moments.

Sometime between these two incidents, I was sitting by the ocean with a young man whom I had been dating for a while. But my thoughts were far away from him. I had come home from a day's teaching to hear the news that my sister's baby had died shortly after birth. After a difficult stop at the hospital, I had met John and retreated to my usual place of comfort, the ocean. John knew how I felt about my sister and the baby, but he was sensitive enough not to push, but to let me sit in silence and just absorb the day's events. I felt lonely and sad, as if I needed to cry but couldn't. Then, as if he knew he had given me aloneness and space long enough, John put his arm around me and held me close. We didn't talk for a long time. There was just silence. I felt understood. And when he told me he loved me later on, I felt a depth we had never shared before.

The college professor went back to grading my papers, and I was the student trying to impress him. My father lapsed into a total unconsciousness from which he never recovered. John and I eventually went two different ways, for, in essence, we were two terribly opposite people. But each for a brief moment during these times provided for the other a moment of

intimacy. For a short time we were on the same wavelength;
we were one.

The poet Matthew Arnold describes that moment when two
people who are, after all, alone in this world touch and become temporarily one:

>Only—but this is rare—
>When a belov'd hand is laid in ours,
>When, jaded with the rush and glare
>Of the interminable hours,
>Our eyes can in another's eyes read clear,
>When our world-deafened ear
>Is by the tones of a loved one caressed—
>A bolt is shot back somewhere in our breast,
>And what we mean, we say, and what we would,
>   we know.
>A man becomes aware of his life's flow,
>And hears its wending murmur, and he sees
>The meadows where it glides, the sun, the
>   breeze.[1]

"A man becomes aware of his life's flow": very often such
an awareness comes after a touch of oneness with another
human being. For not only do we find ourselves in solitude
but we discover much about our being as we touch base with
a like soul. It is perhaps at these peaks of closeness in our
lives that we are least lonely.

Social intimacy is an often misunderstood term. Intimacy is
a word that has been cheapened by a solely sexual connota-
tion, not the deep relationship that should precede it. In essence, intimacy refers to a closeness between two people in
which they become one in mind, emotion, thought and perhaps body. Sexual intercourse should be the peak experience
of an intimate relationship. But, without that relationship, sexual intercourse becomes nothing more or less than can be ac-

complished by two animals in a chance meeting on the street. The important point here is that intimacy may exist in a non-sexual relationship while, at the same time, sexual acts may signify the peak of the intimate relationship. A person's loneliness or lack of it may relate significantly to the amount and quality of the intimacy in his life.

A good parent-child relationship has moments of intimacy. Charles Schulz has a cartoon that appeared years ago depicting a small child asleep in the back seat of a car with words portraying the idea that adulthood means never falling asleep, tired, safe under someone else's care in the back seat of a car. Such a moment in childhood is an act of intimacy. So are talking and stories at bedtime, telling secrets and not being laughed at, being allowed to keep a straggly stray dog and going to sleep with the rain pounding on the roof. For intimacy is safety, security, tenderness with another person. It is a refuge from loneliness.

A patient-doctor type of relationship includes intimacy. A little girl who found it hard to be confronted and afterward crawled into my lap in tears saying, "You hurt me," found intimacy. She was understood and consoled without losing the effectiveness of the recent confrontation. A woman who took twenty minutes to choke out the word "masturbation" and then found she was not condemned found the comfort of intimacy. A businessman who finally found courage to talk about his drug abuse showed relief in having his secret known by one other human being. All of these experiences relate to intimacy, yet none of them include a sexual relationship or even attraction.

Friends of all kinds share this type of closeness from time to time. Normally in any relationship it is not consistently sustained. For, as human beings, we tend to stay within the safety of our self-imposed island living. But, as we have the need, opportunity, and courage, we touch points with another human being and know the joy of intimacy.

For those people who have an intimate relationship that in-

cludes a sexual closeness, all sorts of other details add to that
intimacy, details that would otherwise be ignored. Ruth Calkin lists some in her excellent book for young brides: "The
feel of his strong shoulder when you're achingly weary . . .
the way he tosses his pillow on the floor after he kisses you
good-night . . . the way he reaches for your hand in the quiet
darkness." "Who but you will know," she says. That is intimacy too. And that is a place of shelter from the loneliness
around us.[2]

Intimacy in a relationship cuts through the loneliness of our
human existence because it is always there, available like a
harbor, with its arms open. We may or may not see the person
often, but he or she is there, and that comforts us. She or he
would understand, and that strengthens us. We may become
vulnerable and yet not be exploited. We may be seen at our
best and at our worst and yet be safe from rejection.

A little girl stood at a window looking out at the rain which
was falling gently on the green landscape. Tears were stream-
ing down her face as she watched. Her mother walked into
the room and, not understanding, asked her what was wrong.
"Nothing," she replied; "it's just so beautiful." Satisfied, her
mother left the room. The child was once again alone, with
her enjoyment unmarred by her vulnerability to her mother,
who, while she did not understand, yet did not make the child
feel silly for her sensitivity. Actually, as the mother told me
the story later in the week I sensed a feeling of pride from her
and perhaps even a gentle twinge of envy over this child who
had so much depth of feeling. This child and her mother are
very different in tastes and personality, but they have an enormous amount of mutual trust and respect. That is an intimacy
that allows a person aloneness without the harsher hurt of
deep loneliness.

Yet the very place of safety that an intimate relationship
provides has within it the potential for causing deep feelings
of loneliness. That is the risk of intimacy. A young woman
about to be married discovered that her husband-to-be had

been having an affair with her best friend for several months. The woman's relationship with her fiancé and with her friend had been close and trusting. They had shared happiness as well as some grief. They had enjoyed pleasant times together and encouraged each other's deepest dreams for the future. Now the contrast was almost unbearable. Because the relationship had meant so much, there could only be a huge, lonely void in its place. Because the trust had been deep, the disillusionment was deeper, and it became hard to hold on to the good memories of better days. This is precisely why it is harder to lose an intimate relationship by betrayal than by death itself. For the betrayal of something that was once good and seemingly real shatters even the memories of what once was. In death we can say with the poet Edna St. Vincent Millay:

> Should I outlive this anguish—and men do—
> I shall have only good to say of you.[3]

After betrayal, time can heal much but perhaps rarely to the point of knowing once again the healing touch of all those better times. For what has been deeply positive in our lives has the awesome potential to be equally deeply destructive.

Perhaps no Biblical figure shows us the positive and negative potential of intimacy more than David. David was an extremely sensitive man. His depth of feeling is shown graphically throughout the Book of Psalms. And he is, after all, the only Biblical figure whom God called a man after His own heart, a statement that to me is the supreme compliment of Deity.

David was extremely open to intimacy, as is shown by his sensitivity to the needs of others. For example, in a very perceptive gesture David sent his ambassadors to the new king Hanun, to express his regrets over the death of Hanun's father, who had always been an ally and friend of David's. It was the polite act of one king's well-meaning to another. More

than that, it was David's respect for past loyalty to the son of
the one who had been loyal.

> But Hanun's officers told him, "These men aren't
> here to honor your father! David has sent them to
> spy out the city before attacking it!"
> So Hanun took David's men and shaved off half
> their beards and cut their robes off at the buttocks
> and sent them home half naked. When David heard
> what had happened he told them to stay at Jericho
> until their beards grew out; for the men were very
> embarrassed over their appearance.[4]

It was this kind of sensitivity that made David capable of
forming deep relationships. Even before he was king of Israel
he was loved by the people: ". . . all Israel and Judah loved
him, for he was as one of them."[5] Saul, the king of Israel at
that time, learned to hate David because of David's popularity with the people and because of his power in battle. Yet
Saul's own son, Jonathan, defended David and protected him
in exile. In one touching scene after Jonathan had warned
David of Saul's wrath, "David came out from where he had
been hiding near the south edge of the field and they sadly
shook hands, tears running down their cheeks until David
could weep no more. At last Jonathan said to David, 'Cheer
up, for we have entrusted each other and each other's children into God's hands forever.' So they parted, David going
away and Jonathan returning to the city."[6]
David was vulnerable to hurt as he was open to love. There
is a deep sense of betrayal and consequent loneliness in the
words: "It was not an enemy who taunted me—then I could
have borne it; I could have hidden and escaped. But it was
you, a man like myself, my companion and my friend. What
fellowship we had, what wonderful discussions as we walked
together to the Temple of the Lord on holy days."[7]
Amy Carmichael comments on those who are sensitive to

both love and hurt: "Some are wonderfully created. They can go through a thick flight of stinging arrows and hardly feel them. It is as if they were clad in a fine chain-armour.

"Others are made differently. The arrows pierce, and most sharply if they be shot by friends. The very tone of a voice can depress such a one for a week. (It can uplift too; for the heart that is open to hurt is also very open to love.)"[8]

The "heart that is open to hurt is also very open to love." Somehow that expresses the potential of intimacy with all of its possibilities for feelings of closeness as well as loneliness. Somehow that potential can be a little frightening at times, for when we have been hurt too much we tend to retreat, to "play it safe," to decide not to trust so much again.

Sometimes when I am by the ocean I like to sit on the rocks and watch the tide pools. Tiny fish, crabs, and other creatures have a whole lifetime of activity in just those few inches of shallow water. In an aimless mood I will now and then poke at a sea urchin and watch him retreat quickly back into himself. If I do that several times he just stays there and doesn't come out for a while.

We tend to be like the sea urchin. We become vulnerable and exposed. We lose our sense of loneliness in the contact with a like human being. But then we are suddenly poked at, gently as if with a soft touch or perhaps not so gently as if with a sharp stick. We retreat into the safety of ourselves. If it happens too often, we may retreat for a while away from the vulnerability of intimacy. It is to be hoped that we, too, like the tiny sea urchin, become brave again and come out of our lonely, introverted existence for another chance at intimacy. For it is in close relationships that we find parts of ourselves that we can never find in solitude. We discover a wholeness that we cannot feel while we are totally alone. For just as solitude is important, so is touching base with another human who understands us. Without that experience from time to time, we become truly very lonely human beings.

Ultimately, however, St. Augustine was correct in his idea

that we are made for God and our souls are restless until they find their repose in Him. It is an awesome thought that God originally made man to have fellowship with Him. It is even more awesome that He would go further and at an incredibly high price buy that failing human race back for Himself.

In the depths of man's alienation and loneliness there is the fact: God desires fellowship with man. Herein lies the peak of intimacy and thus the ultimate point of living beyond loneliness. For only with God is there no disillusionment. There are intimacy, vulnerability, exposure. But, while we *do* live in a failing world, we do not have a failing God. Here alone we know perfect intimacy without the chance of betrayal and hurt.

NOTES

1. Matthew Arnold, *The Buried Life*, in Woods and Buckley, *Poetry of the Victorian Period* (New York: Scott, Foresman & Company, 1955), pp. 452–53.

2. Ruth Harms Calkin, *Two Shall Be One* (Elgin, Ill.: David C. Cook Publishing Co., 1977), pp. 127–28.

3. Edna St. Vincent Millay, *Collected Sonnets of Edna St. Vincent Millay* (New York: Washington Square Press, Inc., 1960), XLVII, p. 116.

4. 2 Samuel 10:3–5.

5. 1 Samuel 18:15–16.

6. 1 Samuel 20:41–42.

7. Psalms 55:12–14.

8. Amy Carmichael, *Kohila* (Fort Washington, Pa.: Christian Literature Crusade, n.d.), p. 129.

10

Loneliness
in the Church

"SOMETIMES I JUST go into a church when it's empty and I can be alone and find God," explained Kim, a tenth grader who for some time had been a heroin addict.

I was surprised. I had expected her to sneer at church and God. While I had not expected the ordinary local church to meet her needs, I also had not expected her to find God in an empty church building. "Why empty?" I thought. And yet I knew. For Kim, there had only been rejection from people, even Christian people. But somehow she thought she had a chance with God Himself, and so she had tried to find Him in the empty church building.

For, truly, the organized church, that group of so-called Christians who meet together regularly, often create an atmosphere of loneliness for those who do not conform. By conformity I do not mean agreement even on basic, essential doctrines, but, rather, affirmation of superficial, debatable points.

It is not just the fallen and the weak of this earth who have experienced such isolation. C. S. Lewis, professor of medieval history at Cambridge, commented cryptically on his feelings about the organized church. Lewis does not call himself lonely, because his needs were met in the many class relationships that existed in his life. Yet, as he defines his feelings about churchgoing, they would end up at loneliness if that were his sole source of spiritual and emotional community. Says Lewis unabashedly:

". . . my churchgoing was a merely symbolized and provisional practice. If it in fact helped to move me in the Christian direction, I was and am unaware of this. . . ."

More specifically, ". . . I had as little wish to be in the Church as in the zoo. It was, to begin with, a kind of collective; a wearisome 'get-together' affair. I couldn't see how a concern of that sort should have anything to do with one's spiritual life. To me, religion ought to have been a matter of good men praying alone and meeting by twos and threes to talk of spiritual matters. And then the fussy, time-wasting botheration of it all! the bells, the crowds, the umbrellas, the notices, the bustle, the perpetual arranging and organizing. Hymns were (and are) extremely disagreeable to me. Of all musical instruments I liked (and like) the organ least. I have, too, a sort of spiritual *gaucherie* which makes me unapt to participate in any rite."[1] With Lewis there appear to be no anguished feelings of isolation; simply a taste differing from the average churchgoer.

Joe Bayly, an executive of a publishing company, adds his experience with spiritual isolation when he describes the reactions of some Christians to the death of first his five-year-old and then his teenage son. Here the resulting loneliness is more painful than that of Lewis and a direct result of not being understood by those who should understand.

Says Bayly:

A month or so after our five-year-old died of Leukemia, the same man [previously mentioned in the book]—a sincere, well-educated Christian—told me

that our son need not have died, if we had only pos-
sessed faith.

"Do you really believe that?" I asked.

"Yes, I do," he replied.

"Do you believe it enough to pray that your own
child will become sick with Leukemia so that you
can prove your faith?"

After a long silence, he replied, "No, I don't."

I do not object to such zealots when they are dealing with other adults. I do object to the traumatic
effect they may have on children and teenagers.

The summer after our eighteen-year-old son died,
our sixteen-year-old daughter was at a Christian
camp. A visiting minister, in the presence and with
the silent acquiescence of the camp director, told this
grieving girl, "Your brother need not have died, if
your parents had only had faith for his healing. It is
not God's will for one to die before the age of sixty."

When our daughter told us this in a letter, I
thought about one who died in His early thirties, one
who loved children enough not to hurt them.[2]

This is the epitome of loneliness within organized Christianity. For, because it is where one expects to find the greatest
understanding, the contrast of not being understood or accepted can produce acute feelings of loneliness. Interestingly
enough, I believe that it is more the sincere, the thinkers,
those who follow hard after God, who are at times the most
lonely within the church. For they are the ones who question,
who disagree, and who will not become blind sheep following
a pope-like leader.

One must be careful in such a view not to mistake a search
for truth for arrogance or a difference of opinion for rebellion.
Nevertheless, it is a lonely process in this world to think, to
be, to maintain one's own beliefs.

Dr. Hobart Mowrer, of the University of Illinois, states

that: "One would think that the Church would be a place where people could confront one another openly and honestly, since the Church historically has made no pretense about man's condition and his need for redemption."[3] But Mowrer does not seem to have found it so in his experience.

From a different angle, but reinforcing the lack of understanding and acceptance sometimes found in the church, Viktor Frankl adds: "In former days, people frustrated in their will to meaning would probably have turned to a pastor, priest, or rabbi. Today, they crowd clinics and offices."[4] Thus, again, it is those who search, those who confront themselves, who often feel more lonely in the organized church.

Paul Tournier aptly summarizes the whole viewpoint we have been discussing:

> . . . modern man's loneliness is not the mark of those defeated in life, the sensitive, or the nervous only, but equally of the leaders, of the elite.
>
> We have so effectively preached a "sincerity" in personal convictions that the most devoted people hold themselves back from the crowd and no longer find any community with which they can fully associate themselves. There is always a doctrinal or practical matter to which they cannot sincerely subscribe. They are repulsed by all mass movements and by everything that might be propaganda, and leave these in the hands of shallower minds. This is the great divorce between the elite and the people.
>
> This tragic isolation of the elite is present most acutely in the church, especially in the Protestant Church. Among religious people there are many of a deep spirituality who could and should help the world to awaken to its soul and to put an end to its tremendous moral confusion. However, they move in a world of their own, speak a language of their own, and in their [passion] for sincerity part company

with each other along a thousand different
ways.[5]

Even when they function within the church, "The faithful
sit side by side without even knowing each other; the elders
gather in a little parliament with its parties and formalities;
the pastors do their work without reference to one another."[6]

Again, what is being talked about is the isolation of those
who think, not an elitism of intellectual snobs. We are speaking of genuine individualism, not arrogant, self-centered disagreement. For, indeed, anyone different has a difficult time
with the organized church: the single, widowed, divorced; the
drug addict or alcoholic; a white man in a black church, a
Chicano in a white church; the rich with the poor, or the poor
with the rich. Indeed, to be different within any given group
is to be lonely. We preach the oneness of the Body of Christ
but are horrified when someone different walks in our door.

I remember, when I was a little girl, overhearing a conversation between my parents and their friends as they stood outside the church building.

"I've been trying to convince Mr. Johnson to come to
church," my father said to his friend.

"Oh, he smokes," the friend replied. "We don't want any of
those here."

"Any of those" stuck in my eight-year-old mind. "Any of
those" always meant someone not like us, someone we didn't
want.

Yet, like it or not, we *are* one in the Body of Christ. The
local church, the place where people meet and the people
who meet there, is not the deepest biblical meaning of that
word, church. For, in its truest sense, it refers to that mystical
union of believers in Christ who are joined together in Him.
Such union reaches beyond human discrimination and should
join us here on earth before we are forced together by God
Almighty in Heaven. For the Bible teaches that in that time
many that are last on this earth shall be first, and many that
are first shall be last. Many petty, isolating disagreements will

be dropped, and we may find that we were not always as right as we thought ourselves to be.

Yet, right here now on this earth we do exist as one in God's sight. Practicing that oneness could alleviate much of the loneliness that people experience. My teenage friend on heroin should have been able to find more comfort from a full church than from an empty one.

Since, basically, loneliness is derived from or avoided by the view a person has of himself, his self-image, knowing why we sometimes feel lonely in church, knowing that it may not always be our fault, can at times help minimize the lonely feelings. If I feel good about myself and I am living up to the best of my conscience, then I will not allow the isolation of a local church to affect me so much. I may even get in and try harder to find those people who do not make me feel lonely. And certainly we can find, within the local church and without, people who share a community of beliefs and interests with us.

A friend and I meet almost every Saturday night for dinner, to talk, to pray, to encourage each other in general spiritually and emotionally. We have shared deep things and we know each other well. We can be equally blunt and supportive. And in so doing we have fulfilled in part for ourselves the Corinthians teaching that each member of the Body of Christ is needed by the other and that no member can say to another, "I don't need you." I suppose even those more abrasive members are used by God to sand off our rough edges.

But the Church, the Body of Christ, extends beyond those on this earth. In Hebrews we read a noted list of those men of God who suffered and worked for God in the past. Then the writer of Hebrews, probably Paul, goes on to speak of the large cloud of witnesses who surround us. The Living Bible renders Hebrews 12:1 as follows:

> Since we have such a huge crowd of men of faith watching us from the grandstands, let us strip off anything that slows us down or holds us back. . . .

There are many interpretations of this verse. Some feel that we are just surrounded by the example of great saints of the past. But if we truly believe in a supernatural God, a personal God, a hereafter—and we do—I tend to agree with Amy Carmichael when she speaks of the literal witnesses who observe and encourage us.

Such a view is quite contemporary if one takes at all seriously the accounts of people who have been studied after they "died" and then came back to life. Consistently there seems to have been consciousness in dying, not oblivion.

Sometimes it is in death that the veil between this life and the next seems to open a crack and makes us realize that there is a real, mystical Body of Christ apart from just those who are alive on this earth.

In *A Man Called Peter*, Catherine Marshall illustrates this point very well. After receiving the news of Peter Marshall's death, Catherine Marshall went to the hospital. She describes her experience:

> Later I sat for an hour by Peter's hospital bed. He had been dozing and had slipped away very peacefully.
>
> I felt that I knew just what had happened before I got there. All at once, Peter had *seen* his Lord, and later, his own father, whom he had longed all of his life to know. There had been moments of quiet adoration and of glad reunion. Then suddenly, Peter had realized. He *was dead!*
>
> "You know this will be hard on Catherine," he had said. "What can we do for her?"
>
> And Jesus had smiled at Peter. "She'll be all right. We can supply her with every resource she needs."
>
> So, they had waited for me there. That was why, when I opened the door and stepped quietly into the bare little hospital room, it was filled with the glory of God and with two vivid, transcendent Presences.

Peter was not in the still form, but was hovering near in tenderness and love.

I sat for a long time by the bed holding his hand. After a while there came a gentle tap at the door. It was A.D. I beckoned her to come in. Her eyes seemed glued to my face. Days later, I learned why—what she had seen there. She stayed just a minute, then left.

There came a specific time, exactly fifty minutes by my wrist watch after I had entered the hospital room, when those two luminous Presences left me. Suddenly, the room was empty, cheerless, cold, and I shivered. It was time for me to leave too.

As I rose to go, I knew that this was farewell to the earthly part of this man whom I loved. . . .[7]

"A huge crowd of men of faith watching us from the grandstands. . . ." Literal? I think so. Why, I wonder, do we Christians find it so hard to believe that God is literally just that—GOD! He is not some projection of our imagination or a wishful need fulfillment created in our minds. Whether or not we believe Him has no effect on the truth of His existence. For with or without us He does exist.

When I worked with teenagers on drugs, I encountered manifestations of Satan's reality, occult involvements, that were frighteningly real. I met few Christians who could not believe that the power of the occult was real. I find few Christians who take lightly Hal Lindsey's book on Satan. But we find it so hard to believe that God is by definition supernatural and can therefore act supernaturally. We find it hard to believe in a literal cloud of witnesses while, at the same time, Billy Graham's book *Angels* becomes a best seller. We are, indeed, at best contradictory. Yet to Catherine Marshall on that otherwise grim morning of Peter Marshall's death, the Body of Christ, of which Christ is the Head, provided an alleviation of loneliness. The cloud of witnesses was literal, not just figurative.

Five years ago, I sat at my father's funeral, composed and a little numb. It was early, before the service, and we of the family were seated close to the casket.

Suddenly, as I looked at that cold, metal casket, I felt overwhelmed and alone. After weeks of handling the hospital vigil, I was losing my calm, and death seemed so cold and final.

I forced my glance away from the casket and looked at some of the flowers. They were bright and alive. It was a week before Christmas, so there were numbers of poinsettias, all in full bloom. As suddenly as my composure had been disrupted, a feeling of infinite peace swept over me. He wasn't there. Oh, certainly his body was in that metal box. But *he* wasn't there at all. He was with God and very much alive. My awareness was not substantiated by visions or voices, but I knew on a deep level that he was truly "absent from the body, present with the Lord," probably looking at us at that very moment in compassion over our grief. From that point on I was fine. I had been comforted. I was not alone, as a result of something I had not seen but knew to be true. I had been helped by a part of that cloud of witnesses. It was an important closure for his death. My father had fiercely loved life, so to feel his eternal life present at his funeral was a most appropriate way for God to choose in alleviating my loneliness.

Whether it be in this world or in the next, the Church is to be a source of warmth in a world that can at times feel lonely and even hostile. But we, as imperfect beings in an imperfect world, are, more often than not, lonely if we totally depend on the local church to come through. And so we must learn that in small groups and with individual believers and from God Himself we may find that understanding which helps remove loneliness.

For while self-esteem is the bottom line in handling loneliness, God knows that people can nourish that self-esteem, and that while we each must be born, live, and die alone, yet in fellowship with others we find warmth from the chill and disappointment of life. We share and are shared with, and the pain of life is not carried alone. Joy itself is made more full because others are lifted up by it with us.

> . . . Then it will seem to us that we—we four or five—have chosen one another, the insight of each finding the intrinsic beauty of the rest. . . . In reality, a few years' difference in the dates of our births, a few more miles between certain houses, the choice of one university instead of another—any of these chances might have kept us apart. But, for a Christian there are, strictly speaking, no chances. A secret Master of the Ceremonies has been at work. Christ, who said to the disciples, "Ye have not chosen me, but I have chosen you," can truly say to every group of Christian friends, "You have not chosen one another, but I have chosen you for one another."[8]

To be chosen in Him as a part of the Church as it exists both here and in eternity is to be placed in an honored, responsible position. We dare not say that we have no use for certain members of that Church, that we have no need for them. We dare not isolate those who could benefit from the warmth of our acceptance and love. For, in our desire to avoid loneliness, let us indeed be careful that we are not the cause of other people's loneliness. Then we will ensure that, rather than being a place of acute loneliness for many, the local church will become a place of welcome and refuge. For that is what it was meant to be: not a building that serves people's needs best when it is empty, but a living, vital organism that ministers to a lonely world.

NOTES

1. C. S. Lewis, *Surprised by Joy* (New York: Harcourt, Brace and Company, 1955), p. 234.

2. Joseph Bayly, *The View from a Hearse* (Elgin, Ill.: David C. Cook Publishing Co., 1973), p. 88.

3. O. Hobart Mowrer, *The New Group Therapy* (Princeton, N.J.: D. Van Nostrand Company, Inc., 1964), p. 72.

4. Viktor E. Frankl, *Psychotherapy and Existentialism* (New York: Simon & Schuster, Inc., Publishers, 1968), p. 72.

5. Paul Tournier, *Escape from Loneliness* (Philadelphia: The Westminster Press, 1976), p. 22.

6. Ibid., p. 23.

7. Catherine Marshall, *A Man Called Peter* (New York: McGraw-Hill Book Company, Inc., 1951), pp. 238–39.

8. C. S. Lewis, "The Pleasures of Friendship," *The Saturday Evening Post*, January/February 1979, p. 142, last paragraph.

11

When God Seems Far Away

YESTERDAY WAS A long day. People's problems seemed heavier than usual, and within my own self I felt a kind of deadness that seemed to prevail into the evening. The phone rang. I didn't even feel like answering it, but there is a demanding persistence in the ring of a telephone that is hard to resist.

"Why don't you come over and spend the evening?" said the voice on the other end.

Deadening silence. Then, finally, I agreed, while my thoughts resisted my decision as I remembered how tired I was and how much I didn't want to see anyone. Yet, paradoxically, I felt lonely. I needed someone to give to me.

A few hours later, I was sitting in my friend's living room. We talked and I wondered how he could be so energetic. Then he brought out a record he had found in some remote shop, a British recording of the Choir of King's College, Cambridge. "You'll love this," he said, remembering my passion for old British hymns. As the British tune to "When I Survey the Wondrous Cross" filled the room, I felt transported. The thought went through my mind that heaven, the place of

God's presence, must be magnificent indeed if even a glimmer
of that place can be felt so gloriously on earth. I had felt dry
spiritually. The pain of this world, the tiredness, the pressure
had all reached me. Then, in one breathless moment, all that
had left and I had been refreshed in the presence of God.
Certainly the inspiration of great art, in whatever creative
form it occurs, should never be underestimated.

Dry spells, feelings of spiritual deadness—these occur in the
lives of all of us, for a great variety of reasons. Furthermore,
they have been the experience of persons through all ages.
During the disillusionment of the Industrial Revolution in
England, when God's very existence was being called into
question, Matthew Arnold wrote the famous lines:

> The sea of faith
> Was once, too, at the full, and round earth's shore
> Lay like the folds of a bright girdle furled.
> But now I only hear
> Its melancholy, long, withdrawing roar,
> Retreating, to the breath
> Of the night-wind, down the vast edges drear
> And naked shingles of the world.[1]

During the same century and in the same country, one of
the godliest men of his times, and indeed all times, preached
the following words in a sermon delivered at the Music Hall,
Royal Surrey Gardens, on November 7, 1858:

> It is a rule of the kingdom that all the members
> must be like the head. They are to be like the head
> in that day when he shall appear. "We shall be like
> him, for we shall see him as he is." But we must be
> like the head also in his humiliation, or else we can-
> not be like him in his glory. Now you will observe
> that our Lord and Saviour Jesus Christ very often
> passed through much of trouble without any heavi-

ness. When he said, "Foxes have holes, and the birds
of the air have nests, but the Son of Man hath not
where to lay his head," I observe no heaviness. I do
not think he sighed over that. And when athirst he
sat upon the well, and said, "Give me to drink,"
there was no heaviness in all his thirst. I believe that
through the first years of his ministry, although he
might have suffered some heaviness, he usually
passed over his troubles like a ship floating over the
waves of the sea. But you will remember that at last
the waves of swelling grief came into the vessel; at
last the Saviour himself, though full of patience, was
obliged to say, "My soul is exceeding sorrowful, even
unto death"; and one of the evangelists tells us that
the Saviour "began to be very heavy." What means
that; but that his spirits began to sink? There is more
terrible meaning yet, which I cannot enter into this
morning; but still I may say that the surface meaning
of it is that all his spirits sank within him. He had no
longer his wonted courage, and though he had
strength to say, "Nevertheless, not my will, but thine
be done," still the weakness did prevail, when he
said, "If it be possible let this cup pass from me."
The Saviour passed through the brook, but he
"drank of the brook by the way": and we who pass
through the brook of suffering must drink of it too.
He had to bear the burden, not with his shoulders
omnipotent, but with shoulders that were bending to
the earth beneath a load. And you and I must not always expect a giant faith that can remove mountains: sometimes even to us the grasshopper must be
a burden, that we may in all things be like unto our
head.[2]

In the context of current Christian thinking, periods of feeling distant from God seem connected with sin and failure.

Most people I meet feel guilty when their feelings toward God are dead. This goes back to the "confess your depression" mentality. Certainly, sin does distance one from God, and the feeling of distance is, at times, a warning in each of our lives of something wrong. But what are overlooked too often are the many other reasons for feelings of spiritual deadness.

On the most simple level, spiritual dryness may arise from too little sleep, too much work, physical illness, poor nutrition, and lack of exercise. It is difficult to cultivate a sound spirit in an unsound body. Contrary to the thoughts of some, rest and general restoration of the physical body are vital to spiritual well-being. Once again, to burn out for God sounds highly spiritual, but I'm not at all convinced that this is usually God's plan for our lives. To quote Spurgeon again: "To sit long in one posture, poring over a book, or driving a quill, is in itself a taxing of nature; but add to this a badly ventilated chamber, a body which has long been without muscular exercise, and a heart burdened with many cares, and we have all the elements for preparing a seething cauldron of despair. . . . A day's breathing of fresh air upon the hills, or a few hours' ramble in the beechwoods' umbrageous calm, would sweep the cobwebs out of the brain of scores of our toiling ministers who are now but half alive. A mouthful of salt air, or a stiff walk in the wind's face, would not give grace to the soul, but it would yield oxygen to the body, which is next best."[3] Then, to climax this train of thought, Spurgeon added: "It is economy to gather fresh strength . . . the fisherman [cannot] be always fishing; he must mend his nets. So even our vacation can be one of the duties laid upon us by the kingdom of God."[4]

Perhaps for many of us the sin of spiritual dryness lies not in the feeling but in the exhausting high-wire living that brought us there. Then the depressive feelings are merely God-given signals of the need to refurbish our strength. It is indeed "economy to gather fresh strength."

Yesterday I spoke with a lady who has dedicated her life to a continuous round of activities surrounding church life, children, husband, other people's needs. Recently she has been feeling increasingly tired, irritable and depressed. Her friends are critical of her moods and she feels very lonely. Then guilt sets in—guilt over such feelings and over her "weakness" for having to say no now and then. Yesterday's conversation revolved around her plans for a desperately needed vacation at the beach, which she has almost destroyed already in her plans to center all activities around her three children and three of their friends. She can, and I hope will, have a week of rest combined with a happy time for her children. And in the end they will benefit most from having a calmer, more pleasant mother. But, in her guilt over being human and tired, the mother is almost unable to plan anything for herself. It seems selfish. Yet, what seems self-indulgent to her is called by Spurgeon "one of the duties laid upon us by the kingdom of God."

The concept of distance from God and depressive feelings as they relate to physical weakness is backed up by numerous Biblical examples. Elijah, who was a courageous prophet of God, came to the point where he sat alone in the wilderness after traveling all day and prayed to die. Lonely and exhausted, he gave up.

"'I've had enough,' he told the Lord. 'Take away my life. I've got to die sometime, and it might as well be now.'

"Then he lay down and slept beneath the broom bush."[5]

Wisely, God did not argue with him, for He recognized the physical factors underlying the despair. But He sent an angel who woke him up and commanded him to eat the bread and water he had brought to Elijah. Once again Elijah slept and once again the angel woke him up and forced him to eat. This time "the food gave him enough strength to travel forty days and forty nights to Mount Horeb, the mountain of God. . . ."[6] Then God spoke more to him and gave him instructions. But first God had recognized the priority of the physical in restoring Elijah to a place of service.

Similar stories can be told about men such as Jonah and

Job. And in the New Testament, Christ often met physical needs of healing and hunger before He tried to relate to people on a spiritual level. Nor for Himself did He hesitate at times to go away from the crowds in order to regather His energies.

It is a lonely feeling to experience distance from God. Perhaps that is partly why men such as Elijah begged to die. But if we are merely exhausted, what a comparatively easy cure there is to such spiritual dryness. Yet, how impossible that cure becomes if we spiritualize the physical and go on driving our already tired bodies!

Sometimes the spiritual and emotional factors in our lives combine to bring a feeling of spiritual depression. A person who had experienced much disappointment and loss in past months said to me recently: "Sometimes I feel I have lost God, like He's remote or even angry at me." He feels guilt over such emotions, because they don't seem to be "what other Christians are experiencing." And in his guilt there is a deep loneliness, for distance from God and man is by definition a statement of loneliness.

Depression is an isolating feeling and thus feels distant from God. Anxiety causes feelings of having lost control, of being in danger, and this, too, can create feelings of having lost God. Guilt, even when misguided and unrealistic, creates deep feelings of God's disapproval. Yet, in all of these emotions God *feels* gone. He is not really gone at all. In actuality it is perhaps at these times above all others that God truly desires to be close to us and help us. But too often we put more distance between ourselves and Him by thinking that we have failed and that our feelings of spiritual dryness mean that God has left us. The old hymn says:

> I sought the Lord, and afterward I knew
> He moved my soul to seek Him, seeking me;
> It was not I that found, O Saviour true;
> No, I was found of Thee.[7]

Such words do not refer only to the pursuit by God of those who do not know Him. They also indicate a loving God who desires to draw near to those whom He created when they feel most distant, most alone.

Perhaps the crowning reassurance during periods of spiritual dryness is the knowledge that it is an experience common to those who walk most closely with God. Job, for example, was tested by loss of health, family, wealth, status, friends. Yet this all came about not because of sin but because of Satan's dialogue with God:

> . . . the Lord asked Satan, "Have you noticed my servant Job? He is the finest man in all the earth—a good man who fears God and will have nothing to do with evil."
>
> "Why shouldn't he, when you pay him so well?" Satan scoffed. "You have always protected him and his home and his property from all harm. You have prospered everything he does—look how rich he is! No wonder he 'worships' you! But just take away his wealth, and you'll see him curse you to your face!"
>
> And the Lord replied to Satan, "You may do anything you like with his wealth, but don't harm him physically."[8]

From this time on, Job loses all. No one understands, for it does seem as though Job has indeed come under God's displeasure. Yet, in a deep agony of loneliness, seemingly abandoned by God and man, Job still trusts God in the unseen. Had Job not been so great, Satan would not have wanted to destroy him. And had Job not been so strong, God would not have allowed such a testing. For feelings of distance from God can be a great test of one's real faith in God. And it is a lonely test.

During such times, we are prone to ask what we have done

that is wrong. It might be wise to add to that, "What have I done right that is being tested?" or "What am I about to do that is valuable to God?" or even just "What is the level of my exhaustion at this time?"

For, not only are periods of dryness not always an indication of sinfulness, they are often used as a preparation for further usefulness to God. Dr. J. H. Jowett said it simply: "The world wants to be comforted."[9] And if Thoreau was accurate when he stated that "the mass of men live lives of quiet desperation," then that world that wants comfort will not even begin to relate to a person who has never felt distance from God. To feel such distance is to be human, and to be able to be human is to begin to understand others who walk the same path and feel lonely because no one seems to understand.

On the other hand, there is no need to languish in spiritual depression needlessly. To know the cause is to partially find the cure, a cure that may be no more complicated than a good night's sleep. There are also some general solutions.

A knowledge of God's unchangeableness in the middle of our fluctuating emotions brings hope. To know that God does not change, even though I feel He is changing and becoming more distant, stabilizes me. I enjoy watching the ocean during high tide, when the waves go above the highest rocks surrounding them. During low tide, I like to watch the small creatures in the exposed tide pools, but in my mind is always the certainty of the return of high tide and those magnificent, strong waves. Low times in terms of our emotional responses to God are like the low tide. They come as it comes. But the feelings also leave, just as low tide turns to high tide. God is unchangeable. He is as certain as the return of the high tide. To know *that* in our minds, even though our feelings are totally reversed, will be a help in restoring feelings of closeness to God. To focus on what *is*, rather than what we *feel*, is of vital importance. The security of focus on the known, rather than on the unknown of changing emotions, brings a security that militates against loneliness. For loneliness breeds in the abyss of the unknown.

In determining the cause of spiritual depression, a sense of good self-worth is of great importance. Some people are always sure they're wrong, even when they're very right. To such a person, any glimmer of distance from God is interpreted as a result of sin. This is why a good self-image is so very important, for it makes a person secure enough to admit he's wrong and courageous enough to be sure when he's right. Knowing that the cause of one's spiritual depression is not sin enables a person to look more perceptively at the cause or causes and thus to work productively through to a solution.

Several years ago, when I had just recently started my private practice in counseling, I began to get feelings of dissatisfaction and boredom. But I kept on going as though they didn't exist. Then, one day in my office, a child I was very interested in came for her appointment. My spontaneous, immediate reaction was indifference. At the end of the day, when I had time to reflect upon my feelings, I realized that I had been going nonstop for two years with no break. Of course, I felt indifferent about the needs of others when I was so exhausted I was hardly surviving myself. My solution was a week at the ocean, which greatly restored me. God seemed near again. I cared about my work, and I was enthusiastic once more. Yet, had I spiritualized my exhaustion out of a sense of self-hate, I would have felt guilty about my indifference, felt further than ever from God and been lonely in my isolation from God and man. Worst of all, in my guilt I would have worked harder than ever, rather than stopping to rest.

In general there are probably as many helps to getting over dry spells as there are people. Small, trivial things can be uplifting to some of us: candles and glass candle holders; a walk in some beautiful spot—for me, by the ocean; dinner out with a close friend; a day set aside for doing something special for oneself; a new devotional book—or the renewal of acquaintance with an old one; ancient hymns—or new ones if that is more appealing; any music that appeals and uplifts. Moods are incredibly changeable, even moods that relate to God. And so the trivial should not be overlooked.

Deeper solutions must be suited to the cause of the dead, stale feelings. Still, the most basic factor of all is the realization that dry spells are not always a sign of God's disapproval and our failure. There is no lonelier position than that in which one feels isolated from God and then is made to believe that the feeling is a result of sin and God's consequent wrath.

When we as Christians see someone whose life is enduring great loss and pain, we tend at least to think, if not to ask: Where has he sinned? What has he done to deserve such pain? We might more lovingly and constructively ask, "For what end is this man's life being tested? For what great work is he being prepared?" For under such testing it is indeed often accurate to say, "Here is a person whom God can trust, and here is a person whom God will use."

NOTES

1. Matthew Arnold, *Dover Beach*, in Woods and Buckley, *Poetry of the Victorian Period* (New York: Scott, Foresman & Company, 1955), p. 483.

2. Charles H. Spurgeon, *The New Park Street Pulpit* (London: The Banner of Truth Trust, 1964), Vol. 4, p. 460.

3. Helmut Thielicke, *Encounter with Spurgeon*, transl. by John W. Doberstein (Grand Rapids, Mich.: Baker Book House, 1975 reprint), pp. 217–18.

4. Ibid., p. 11.

5. 1 Kings 19:4–5.

6. 1 Kings 19:8.

7. Paul Beckwith, compiler and editor, *The Hymnal of Inter-Varsity Christian Fellowship* (Chicago: Inter-Varsity Press, 1969 reprint), p. 78.

8. Job 1:8–13.

9. Richard E. Day, *The Shadow of the Broad Brim* (Philadelphia: Judson Press, 1934), p. 173.

12

What We All Really Seek

THIS WAS DEFINITELY not just the *"turista."* The fever, the weakness, the pain in the wrong places, all implied something a little more severe than the usual "Montezuma's revenge," so common to tourists in Mexico. I had spent four beautiful, quiet days in a little fishing village in Mexico and now I was flat in bed. In two days I faced a long, hot drive to Acapulco, which was one hundred and fifty miles away, then a flight home to California. Yet now I was too weak even to go to the hotel dining room for lunch!

During the early part of the day, I wavered in and out of sleep. It felt good to sleep, even though I had vague fears about being so sick in such a remote place. It crossed my mind more than once that if I got sick enough to require medical attention, it would be hours before I could get to either Mexico City or Acapulco. And above all, with my allergies I would be in real life-threatening danger if someone gave me any medicine to which I was allergic. I had experienced anaphylactic shock once in my life, when the internal swelling from an allergy-producing substance created an inability to breathe, and I wasn't anxious to experience that feeling ever again.

Then, toward afternoon, I found myself feeling very peaceful indeed about God's ability to take care of me. My loneliness from being sick in a remote part of the world left, and I prayed for God to heal me. I remember feeling that my prayer was especially legitimate for two reasons: first, God had already made it plain to me that He had a plan for my life, a plan that had not yet been fulfilled; and second, medical help was not readily available to me.

I went back to sleep, this time into a more relaxed rest. By evening I was able to go to the hotel dining room to eat—shakily! And by the next day I resumed most of my normal vacation activities.

I cannot in detail explain my experience of that day. I can only say that in the midst of much potential fear and loneliness, God was there and met my needs. When most else failed, there was God.

Loneliness is an emotion that God understands, and at times He fills that empty, scary feeling with Himself. Yet, as we have noted repeatedly, loneliness is not sick or strange or pathological. It is part of being human, and as such it cannot be eradicated. We are human and hate pain. Understandably, therefore, we try to eradicate that pain, but it doesn't work. Loneliness is like the tide of the sea. It ebbs and flows, recedes and comes in. Indeed, all emotion is that way, for no feeling remains constant. The next time you are happy, grasp that feeling, hold it, preserve it, concentrate on it—and you will see it vanish. For no emotion can be trapped, any more than the ebbing tide can be contained and controlled within man-made walls.

But we can learn to handle, control, and even grow through our emotions, both positive and negative. Loneliness is like every other feeling. It cannot be stamped out, but it can be used positively. In Mexico I learned to trust God in a deeper way through my loneliness, and I found what the poet Whittier discovered years ago when he wrote of blindly trusting God and finding the Rock beneath. Therefore the experience was not wasted.

For in essence we are always alone in this life, if not lonely. In referring to the increased individualized identity of women, Anne Morrow Lindbergh speaks of aloneness in one's person as a positive quality:

> . . . With growth, it is true, comes differentiation and separation, in the sense that the unity of the tree trunk differentiates as it grows and spreads into limbs, branches, and leaves. But the tree is still one, and its different and separate parts contribute to one another. The two separate worlds or the two solitudes will surely have more to give each other than when each was a meager half. "A complete sharing between two people is an impossibility," writes Rilke, "and whenever it seems, nevertheless, to exist, it is a narrowing, a mutual agreement which robs either one member or both of his fullest freedom and development. But once the realization is accepted that, even between the closest human beings, infinite distances continue to exist, a wonderful living side by side can grow up, if they succeed in loving the distance between them which makes it possible for each to see the other whole and against a wide sky!"[1]

And sometimes loneliness itself is simply a feeling that must be partially endured.

In my office I see the loneliness of those with emotional problems, who, in addition to solving these problems, must sometimes cope with isolation from friends and family who don't understand. Even children feel the loneliness of being different. As one ten-year-old said to me, "I'm not like everyone else, am I? So I know I need to see you." I had hoped she hadn't noticed how different she was, but she was too bright not to notice.

Old age is another aspect of loneliness that is increasingly acute in this country. Enforced retirement, which removes one's task, and the rejection of being shunted off to a convalescent home have a drastic negative effect on a person's self-image. The result is acute loneliness.

The loneliness of being right when no one else thinks you are; the loneliness experienced in losing a loved one; the loneliness of so-called failure—these are other forms of loneliness that cannot immediately be gotten rid of, but they can have meaning in our lives, and that lessens and eventually alleviates the loneliness.

Amy Carmichael well described a positive use of pain when she wrote:

> Before the winds that blow do cease
> Teach me to dwell within thy calm.[2]

It is what we are *while* the winds are blowing that gives pain meaning. And the more we find meaning in our loneliness, the more our self-image will rise, since we have not allowed the loneliness to harm us. This in turn tends to actually alleviate and eventually take away the lonely feelings. For, when I feel good about myself, I will not feel as lonely as I do when I am down on myself. In this sense, loneliness, while it does exist for us all, does not need to be overwhelming. Part of the success of handling loneliness lies in understanding and anticipating its occurrence.

When I was little, I had a dentist who always warned me when his drill was going to hurt. And it never seemed to hurt as much as he said it would. In contrast, my pediatrician, who assured me that shots never hurt, sent me into a fear of needles that lasted through college! He may have thought it didn't hurt, but I knew better!

In the same way, if we expect no loneliness, no pain in life,

BEYOND LONELINESS

—and they will be. But if we accept loneliness as inevitable,
yet controllable and alterable, we will find meaning in our
suffering and grow from our experience. In short, we will not
be disillusioned by life and we will become stronger for it.

Such a thought is not new. Indeed, what is new is the Western world's notion that all pain is pathological and that we
should be able to eradicate that pain and live happily ever
after.

The nineteeth-century philosopher Thomas Carlyle wrote
an entire book, *Sartor Resartus*, on the concept that if you re-
duce your expectations to zero, then anything you get is happiness, since it is at that point unexpected. Rather than trying
to eradicate pain, Carlyle was almost extreme in feeling that
most of life is not *up, up, up*. The Christian view is more positive, but no real Bible scholar would support the notion that
Christianity eradicates pain and loneliness.

Indeed, the Psalms are a living testimony to a different concept. David is frequently lonely. In a loneliness arising from
standing alone for right, David cries:

> When will you comfort me with your help? I am
> shriveled like a wineskin in the smoke, exhausted
> with waiting. But still I cling to your laws and obey
> them. How long must I wait before you punish those
> who persecute me? . . . Help me, for you love only
> truth. . . . (Psalm 119:82–86.)

David is in the depths of loneliness. Even rightness and
meaning do not eradicate his feelings. Yet, not much later he
can say:

> Shall I look to the mountain gods for help? No! My
> help is from Jehovah who made the mountains! And
> the heavens too! He will never let me stumble, slip or

fall. For he is always watching, never sleeping.
(Psalm 121:1-4.)

Loneliness? Yes! Eradication? No! Alleviation and ultimate
meaning? Yes! That is our balance. Not drowning in loneliness.
Not eradicating it. But handling it. Therein are health and
godliness. Therein are reality as well as peace.

"A 'Bridge Over Troubled Water'—isn't that what we're all
here for?" That was the question my photographer friend
asked us in that restaurant on the hill overlooking a Mexican
bay. Yes and no. Sure, we were trying to escape the rat race of
American life. We were seeking in each other an honesty and
a closeness that would alleviate the loneliness we all feel from
time to time. But as I have thought about it since, I have
come to a gut-level realization that to live beyond loneliness is
not to bury one's feelings in busyness or to run to an exotic
resort, not even the enchanting Zihuatanejo Bay. It is to be
found within one's own self, within that core of self-
confidence that accepts oneself and is comfortable with oneself. It is to be found in the positiveness of a task and the reality of one's Taskmaster. It is to be found in quietness in one's
own backyard. It is not for sale, cannot be bartered for or ne-
gotiated. Yet, to live beyond loneliness is a state for which
kings would exchange their power and fortunes. For it is what
we all really seek.

NOTES

1. Anne Morrow Lindbergh, *Gift from the Sea* (New York: The
New American Library, 1961), p. 95.

2. Amy Carmichael, *Rose from Briar* (Fort Washington, Pa.:
Christian Literature Crusade, 1973), p. 12.

Bibliography

BAYLY, JOSEPH. *The View from a Hearse.* Elgin, Ill.: David C. Cook Publishing Co., 1973.

CALKIN, RUTH HARMS. *Lord, I Keep Running Back to You.* Wheaton, Ill.: Tyndale House Publishers, Inc., 1979.

———. *Tell Me Again, Lord, I Forget.* Elgin, Ill.: David C. Cook Publishing Co., 1974.

———. *Two Shall Be One.* Elgin, Ill.: David C. Cook Publishing Co., 1977.

CARMICHAEL, AMY. *Gold by Moonlight.* Fort Washington, Pa.: Christian Literature Crusade, 1970.

———. *Gold Cord.* Fort Washington, Pa.: Christian Literature Crusade, 1932.

———. *Kohila.* Fort Washington, Pa.: Christian Literature Crusade, n.d.

DAY, RICHARD E. *The Shadow of the Broad Brim.* Philadelphia: Judson Press, 1934.

FABRY, JOSEPH B. *The Pursuit of Meaning.* Boston: Beacon Press, Inc., 1968.

FRANKL, VIKTOR E. *Man's Search for Meaning.* New York: Simon & Schuster, Inc., Publishers, 1959.

———. *Psychotherapy and Existentialism.* New York: Simon & Schuster, Inc., Publishers, 1968.

———. *The Doctor and the Soul.* New York: Vintage Books, 1973.

———. *The Will to Meaning.* New York: The World Publishing Company, 1969.

GUINNESS, JOY. *Mrs. Howard Taylor, Her Web of Time.* London agents: Lutterworth Press; China Inland Mission, 1952 reprint.

HOUGHTON, FRANK. *Amy Carmichael of Dohnavur.* Fort Washington, Pa.: Christian Literature Crusade, n.d.

HUGHES, HUGH PRICE. *The Journal of John Wesley.* Chicago: Moody Press, 1974.

LEWIS, C. S. *Letters to an American Lady.* Grand Rapids, Mich.: William B. Eerdmans Publishing Company, 1971.

———. *Mere Christianity.* London: Geoffrey Bles, Ltd., 1962.

———. *Surprised by Joy.* New York: Harcourt, Brace and Company, 1955.

———. *The Problem of Pain.* New York: The Macmillan Company, 1962.

LINDBERGH, ANNE MORROW. *Gift from the Sea.* New York: The New American Library, 1961.

MARSHALL, CATHERINE. *Beyond Ourselves.* New York: Avon Books, 1961.

———. *A Man Called Peter.* New York: McGraw-Hill Book Company, Inc., 1951.

MAY, ROLLO. *Man's Search for Himself.* New York: W. W. Norton & Company, Inc., Publishers, 1953.

MILLAY, EDNA ST. VINCENT. *Collected Sonnets of Edna St. Vincent Millay.* New York: Washington Square Press, Inc., 1960.

MOWRER, O. HOBART. *The New Group Therapy.* Princeton, N.J.: D. Van Nostrand Company, Inc., 1964.

SKOGLUND, ELIZABETH R. *Loving Begins with Me.* New York: Harper & Row, Publishers, 1979.

——. *To Anger, with Love.* New York: Harper & Row, Publishers, 1977.

——. *Where Do I Go to Buy Happiness?* Downers Grove, Ill.: Inter-Varsity Press, 1972.

SMALLEY, DONALD, ed. *Poems of Robert Browning.* Boston: Houghton Mifflin Company, 1956.

SPURGEON, CHARLES H. *The New Park Street Pulpit.* London: The Banner of Truth Trust, 1964.

THIELICKE, HELMUT. *Encounter with Spurgeon,* transl. by John W. Doberstein. Grand Rapids, Mich.: Baker Book House, 1975 reprint.

TOURNIER, PAUL. *A Place for You.* New York: Harper & Row, Publishers, 1968.

——. *Guilt and Grace.* New York: Harper & Row, Publishers, 1962.

——. *Escape from Loneliness.* Philadelphia: The Westminster Press, 1976.

TURNBULL, COLIN M. *The Mountain People.* New York: Simon & Schuster, Inc., Pubs., 1972.